HEARTS FOREVER YOUNG

The Journey Continues

Ann McColl Lindsay

Photographs by David Lindsay

Library and Archives Canada Cataloguing in Publication

CIP data on file with the National Library and Archives

ISBN 978-1-55483-923-0

To independent book stores.

HEARTS FOREVER YOUNG

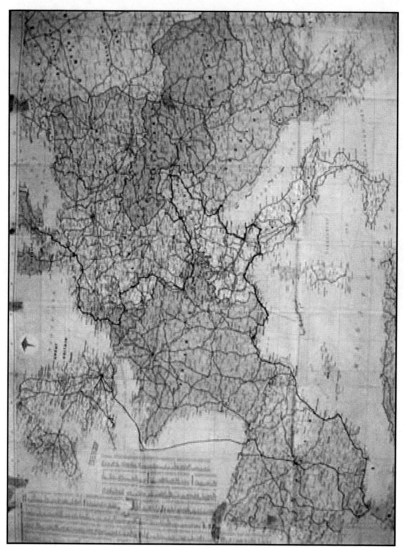

Route map: The van followed the black line.

Prologue

A FRENCH AFFAIR
For better or for worse

March, 2010 NICE

Slivers of light filter through the wooden slats of the shuttered arched window, casting a tropical air over this white bedroom near the *Promenade des Anglais*. An appropriate setting for the raging fever that has kept me confined for three days and nights. I sit in bed admiring the elaborate plaster crown moulding, the crystal chandelier and all the details of the furnishings, because I can't breathe when I lie down. This bronchial attack is the latest in a forty-year litany of illnesses that have plagued our trips to France. We're not the only ones. The cemeteries along the Mediterranean coast are filled with tubercular English writers who flocked here hoping for a cure.

My confinement allowed time for me to ask myself, Why do we keep coming back to France? I found the answer in the lines from the traditional marriage ceremony: *For better or worse, in sickness and in health, till death us do part* ....which perfectly describe my long-term relationship with France. It is a relationship based on love - of the French people, the land, its culture. Despite foul weather on most visits and serious bouts of food poisoning, sprained ankles, and lactose intolerance more times than enough, we have remained faithful to this country since first crossing the border from Spain in our twenties.

CROSSING THE BORDER

The first six months of our trip, described in *Hungry Hearts - A Food Odyssey across Britain and Spain 1968 - 69*, covered three countries, Scotland, England and Spain, leaving the reader at the French border. This second volume includes the remaining eight countries - France, Italy, Austria, Switzerland, Germany, Belgium, the Netherlands, and Denmark.

In the summer of 1968 David and I resigned from teaching, sold our house and furniture, cashed in savings and made plans to spend every cent on a year's camping in Europe. Besides being fun, it was life-changing. September in Scotland introduced us to historic kitchens in manor houses, small independent grocers, and antique stores jammed with domestic serving pieces. On our run down to the south coast of England, the van became a stockroom of pedigree utensils that hardly qualified as essential camping gear. A china ham stand from a butcher's shop in Nevis, a carved bread board and knife from Sheffield, a pair of ridged butter hands from a farm store, a silver cake stand from a jumble sale in the crypt of a church. They all told a story about a lost way of preparing and serving food, filling a gap in our sketchy culinary pasts. When we reached the south coast, we perched outside the van on the cliffs of Dover and picnicked on ham, bread, butter and cakes from the correct serving pieces. But I still could not cook.

By the time we crossed the Bay of Biscay, en route to Spain in January 1969, my reading material had changed from the English classics to Elizabeth David's *Mediterranean Food*. Autumn in Britain had covered early kitchen architecture. Spain provided a hands-on class in food-prep; an immersion in the smells, tastes, sunshine and earthiness of *cucina del pueblo.* On a beach in Alicante, I decided to open a kitchen shop when we returned home. I had yet to learn how to use the tools of the trade, but we were in the right spot. France and Italy had the raw ingredients and the impressive culinary legacies necessary for instruction on the next chapter of this personal journey. That border crossing was as significant for us as the Rubicon.

Our marriage with France started, as do most other marriages, on too tight a budget. We crossed the border from Spain, intending to spend March in France in a camper van, with the warnings of other young road travellers echoing in our ears, "Watch every penny in France. It is ruinously expensive. They dare to charge seventy cents for two coffees at an outdoor café." We were silly enough to believe that only by exercising extreme budgetary caution, could we pass along the Riviera, playground of the rich and famous, without becoming bankrupt. Another experienced camper advised us to stock up on staple groceries before leaving Barcelona. Sheer folly, but we actually did this. The purse stayed firmly closed for the twelve mile run into France, past souvenir vendors lining the road up to the Pyrennes with their tempting Spanish pottery.

Our biggest mistake was rushing through France. Couples in the first decade of a relationship have a tendency to see everything quickly. On subsequent trips, this haste has been replaced by leisurely months in an apartment in one place, a necessary comfort for the ailing.

Forward Flashes

In this book, I have chosen to temper my 1969 journal accounts of whirlwind living in a van from one camp site to the next in one day, by fast-forwarding to richer memories of more languorous later visits.

FRANCE
The Marketplace
February 28, 1969 PERPIGNAN

The decrease in the number of Spanish civil guards and the increase in the number of sports cars, indicated that we had arrived in Perpignan, France. First stop was a large grocery store whose delicatessen counters were stocked with pâtés and cheeses next to chickens roasting on spits, and a bakery counter that made us want to throw away the frugal bag of groceries we had carted across the border. The conversations between customers and across the counter, centered on the appropriateness of specific ingredients for a particular recipe, the correct joint, cut, or wedge that would suit the evening meal. Even with rudimentary French, we knew that we had entered a country very concerned about food in all its stages.

We began to understand the deep-rooted awareness and appreciation of food as a cultural component, along with flowers, art, architecture and landscape. Meals are not based on the cheapest, the quickest, or the easiest.

Within our first week in France, we observed three basic cornerstones of meal preparation in a country that has a high reputation for getting the food to the table:
- search out sources of high quality prepared dishes
- shop at street markets loaded with fresh local ingredients
- use traditional utensils and methods

This grocery store was our first eye-opener. The French housewife had access to "take-out" of a high quality, a real boon for those limited to a camper van burner. The "fast food" available in the store we visited in 1969 was healthy. It differed from the processed truckloads prepared in industrialized kitchens in that it was made locally, fresh daily, did not contain additives or preservatives and was not vacuum packed. Most prepared foods were to be found in *charcuteries*, butcher shops with dizzying selections of cured hams, spiced sausages, game terrines, country *pâtés*. Special butchers, called *traiteurs*, offered a cooler filled with glass bowls of wild rice mixed with cranberries, couscous salad, cooked paella or white bean *cassoulet*. Van dinners became more substantial with the roasted cuts of pork loin, chops and ham *persil* wrapped up for the asking. Picnic lunches on beaches or under the trees became adventures in good eating with soft and hard cheeses, grain and bean salads, and perfectly ripened fruits. This country was a campers' paradise.

The French housewife gathers knowledge of reputable provisioners - the best *pâtisseries*, where she can rely on finding a perfect tart for a dinner party; the nearest traditional *boulanger* who continues to bake crusty *baguettes bien cuite*; exquisite chocolate shops and *confiseries* for the special desserts. Since a typical family meal can stretch through long sessions at the table - soup, main, salad, cheese, dessert - one of the little *trucs* of the home cook is to rely on her provisioners. The skill is in choosing well, particularly in the *fromageries*, where a dizzying array of cheeses in various degrees of ripeness, need to be assessed for immediate consumption. We really had no need to cook while in France, but the number two national bastion of fine food - the street markets - made it impossible to resist. If I could keep a good vinaigrette on hand in the van, we would only have to pick up fresh lettuces and vegetables to prepare a meal.

VARIATIONS ON THE THEME OF VINAIGRETTE

The first challenge was to find white vinegar, which I considered essential. Wrong, according to all store clerks interviewed. The French prefer red wine vinegar so that's what the stores mainly stock. You can use white or lemon juice, but the red does give a classic depth and finish to the dressing. Use other lighter vinegars for very delicate salad greens or as a dressing on cold fish. Extra virgin olive oil is the standard. All ingredients should be of high quality and recently purchased - stale or rancid will ruin a bowl of garden greens.

The proportion of vinegar to oil varies according to taste from 1 to 3 to 1 to 8. We prefer the high end of the ratio: 1 tablespoon acidic to 6 of oil for a fruity, smooth dressing.

INGREDIENTS
2 teaspoons Dijon mustard
1/2 teaspoon sea salt
2 turns of the pepper mill
1 tablespoon red wine vinegar
6 tablespoons olive oil

METHOD
1. The chef at La Varenne instructed us (in the 1980s) to place the mustard in the bottom of a glass salad bowl.
   Whisk in the salt, pepper and vinegar with a small wire whisk.
2. Dribble in the oil one tablespoon at a time, whisking continuously to make a smooth emulsion.

3. Pour into a small bottle which has a screw top or cork seal. Use within a week.
4. At home, I follow the same procedure, but mix in a glass measure so that I can more easily pour the resulting dressing into a storage jar.

This dressing is worth the expense of fine ingredients because it has many more uses than dressing a salad:

> Use it in place of butter over warm vegetables such as cauliflower and broccoli.
> Dribble on asparagus spears.
> Coat cold fish or chicken.
> Dress mini shrimp in an avocado half.
> Marinate mushrooms.

Fresh herbs such as tarragon, coriander, parsley, mint, lovage, lemon balm, basil, chives, and/or dill should be added at the time of preparation to suit the ingredients. Resist shaking them into the dressing as it is being made.

CREAMY CRUDITÉS

This dressing is simplicity itself, but indispensible for creating a crudité plate.

INGREDIENTS
dressing:
1/4 cup 18% cream
2 teaspoons Dijon mustard
1/2 teaspoon sea salt
2 grinds of pepper

select four or five of these vegetables:
fennel bulb
celery root
celery stalk
radish
cauliflower
broccoli
bok choy
carrots
fresh sweet peas
small tomatoes

METHOD
1. Whisk the seasonings and mustard into the cream.
2. Slice, dice, grate or shred the veg of choice.
3. Toss each separately in a bowl with either the vinaigrette or the

cream dressing, according to taste.

4. You can substitute creamed horseradish for the mustard if you prefer more variety.

5. Arrange small mounds of the dressed vegetables around each plate.

A typical café in the south of France.

Perpignan, with its gaily painted shops, Arab quarter perfumed with spices, and lively beach scene, taught us to expect an eclectic mix along the Med. Architectural treasures, such as a triple fireplace in the great hall of *le Palais des Rois de Majorque*, exist beside tourist draws of sun and sand. From the tower of this palace, we could see a beach to camp on and mountains to be crossed. Part of the 14th century town gate now contains a museum honouring Catalan glazed terracotta kitchen pots. A neighbouring bistro was serving generous-sized earthenware bowls of green lentils with a sausage on top. We searched out a grocer whose cooler displayed large glass bowls filled with prepared salads. I pointed to the bistro's special and asked for an explanation.

"*Lentilles du Puy* are recognized by their deep green-black colour and their intensity of flavour, due to their *terroir*, the volcanic soil of the Auvergne in central France."

He packed us a pint container of lentils, simmered in herbs and vegetables, for our initial low-cost, high-protein French meal to enjoy with chunks of bread by candlelight in the van.

BISTRO LENTILS

This recipe includes the vegetables and herbs I could recognize in our take-away version. In addition, we simmer a coil of garlic sausage in a separate pot to serve alongside the lentils.

INGREDIENTS

1 cup of French lentils from the Puy region, rinsed (should serve four)

2 cups of herbal or vegetable broth including a few sprigs of fresh thyme and a bay leaf

1 extra cup of liquid to be added later if needed

1 large clove of garlic, peeled and crushed

1 teaspoon coarse sea or kosher salt

3 grinds of black pepper

1 onion, chopped

2 small firm carrots, diced (1/2 cup)

1 stalk of celery, halved lengthwise and sliced

2 tablespoons red or sherry vinegar

2/3 cup of olive oil

1 tablespoon granular Dijon mustard

METHOD

1. Simmer the lentils in the broth with the salt, pepper, thyme, bay and garlic for 20 minutes.

2. If you are serving with sausage, start it to simmer at the same time, in a covered skillet with enough water to cover the sausage.

3. Add the onions, carrots and celery to the lentils after the 20 minutes, with the extra cup of broth or water if needed, to bring the liquid

up to the top of the mixture.

4. Simmer for an additional 10 to 15 minutes, until the lentils and vegetables are tender but not mushy.

5. In a small bowl, whisk the mustard into the vinegar. Incorporate the olive oil.

6. Remove the lentil mixture from the burner. Drain if too moist. Take out thyme branches and bay leaf. Stir in the vinaigrette. Allow to cool to room temperature in a bowl.

7. Serve with a section of sausage, a garnish of parsley, a pot of Dijon and a thick piece of rye bread.

Street life along the coast continued our grounding in ingredients, food preparation and presentation that were a natural prologue to a career in supplying the food industry. The trip was becoming a long chain of taste memories. I cannot remember being impressed by any hardware stores in our journey along the French coast. As a matter of fact, I don't think we went into any, and I know for certain that we didn't shop for cookware, the third tenet for the success of French cooking.

The retailers that I admire most, Elizabeth David and Terence Conran, have both written lyrically about the masses of pottery and bakeware they had discovered in French warehouses and loaded into trucks for their stores in England. We were not yet in a position to buy French cookware, but I had come to value tools for their sensual appeal, like the satin wood graining on even such ordinary household items as wooden spoons. A beechwood stirrer was highly polished to give a smooth, impervious finish. Generally, a fine ridge was cut a few centimeters up from the end of the handle, for no other reason than to add a finishing touch. Then again, a housewife could tie a string around this groove to hang the spoon on a hook near the stove. Care had been expended on the simplest details of a kitchen tool. The elegance of wire baskets for egg storage, the depth of a chocolate brown glaze inside a beige jug, all heightened a sensual learning curve. Or as Proust phrased it, *Chardin has taught us that a pear is as living as a woman, a kitchen crock as beautiful as an emerald.* Although I did not buy any cookware in France, I had absorbed some of the art involved in cooking with care and eating well.

March 1, 1969 SÈTE

After a month of sunny days in Spain, we expected spring to follow us. Instead we entered the eye of a storm. The landscape changed. Plane trees rather than palms formed an arch over many of the roads, and vineyards replaced olive groves as we followed the coastal roads toward the *Golfe du Lion*. Monsoons dogged our attempts to picnic by the harbour in Sète, a serious fishing port on the gulf. Parked amongst blowing sand dunes and grey breakers, we seemed to be back in St. Andrews on the North Sea. But in this city, bustling with captains and sailors buying boat parts from the crammed nautical suppliers, you have many warm, dry choices of eateries, all of them offering oysters, mussels and other treasures that were in the sea an hour earlier. We struggled with umbrellas along the quay before turning into one of the fishermen's haunts for our first slurp of fresh oysters from their shell. They are eaten plain - no seafood sauce, no chopped onion, no vinegar, no capers - just a pure hit of the briny deep. The barman wielding a stout, blunt oyster opener, inserting it in just behind the hinge, twisting deftly, gave us all the instruction a retailer would need to sell that tool.

March 1, 1969 NÎMES

We entered the city, windshield wipers going full speed, through one of the four arches of the *Porte Auguste*, once part of an extensive Roman wall. Veterans of the Roman Legions who served with Caesar in his Nile campaigns were given plots of land to cultivate on the plains surrounding the city; a crocodile chained to a palm tree is this city's coat of arms. Situated just north of Arles, and west of Avignon, Nîmes was a crossroads for the Roman legions, who left southern France with an impressive assortment of significant buildings. Pity we could not enjoy them on that first trip. Rain poured through the first century stone arches of *Les Arènes*, the still-intact ampitheatre where 25,000 could watch lions emerge from tunnels to tackle Christians. Opera lovers fill the stone benches now on concert nights.

Brollies raised, we gamely forged on to *La Maison Carrée*, a uniquely intact square temple of Corinthian columns through which rain whistled. The Emperor Agrippa dedicated it to his sons in 2 AD and it remains the best preserved of Rome's temples. We sheltered in front of the huge wooden doors, flanked by a pair of impressive clay urns, under the sculpted frieze of the portico. The sturdy blue cloth, woven in Nîmes and therefore named denim (de Nîmes), would have been a better clothing choice for the weather than our woollens, now soggy and with little chance of drying in the mouldy van. We skipped the Castellum, the main ancient aqueduct which received water from the nearby *Pont du Gard* and distributed it to the narrow streets of the city. Not the right day to view a water works. But we did walk across the two thousand year-old *Pont du Gard* a few days later when the sun came out.

We came back to this area years later when a friend loaned us a tiny restored farmhouse with a big stove. Even though it was also the month of March, copious sunshine, four gas burners and an oven, allowed us to cook with the herbs, fruits and vegetables found in the many fine surrounding markets. These colourful trading places have their roots in pre-Roman times. Close by the Greek *stoa* (colonnaded meeting place) was the *agora* (marketplace). In marketplaces around the world ideas continue to be traded along with coin and produce. Most of the markets in Provence are twisting rows of canopies that choke the streets with pedestrians, funnelling everyone down to a climatic meeting place. In Uzès, it is the circle of olive stalls that surrounds the elegant stone fountain in the *Place aux Herbes*. In Nîmes, the vendors of lavender, lentils, couscous and honey branch out from the sacred spring which marks the pre-Roman foundation of the city. *Blvd. Jean Jaurès* runs along the *Jardin de la Fontaine*, a garden of beautiful sculpture and trees constructed at the site of the ancient spring and dedicated to *Nemausus*, the river god. The key element of a market is the *genus loci*, or spirit of the place, which overflows its confines and embraces the locality with lust and life. We search for this market magic in every city we have visited.

Outside the Hania market in Crète, Greek men sip ouzo under olive trees; the scent of coffee and almonds fills the square. Outside the simple whitewashed market building in Nerja, Spain, they sip sherry under orange trees while fishermen hawk crustaceans from marble slabs. The pavements fringing Barcelona's market ring with bird song and the scent of flower stalls. It seems as though market buildings cannot contain earth's bounty - it floods onto the sidewalks creating street bazaars that breed sociability.

On our first attempt to find the market in Nîmes, we found ourselves in the middle of a full-scale carnival that had taken over the streets for that day. Ferris wheels and car rides had replaced the leeks and berries. But this was just temporary. Most of the time, the city comes alive with vendors' cries from stalls piled with the fruit and vegetables of Provence, as this journal entry records:

La Maison Carrée, a second century temple, is one of the best preserved
Roman antiquities in a city that boasts many.

"Up and out to a market in full swing this morning. Fresh an-chovies to grill and rabbit to stew. Pots of mint and tarragon to add flavour. Litres of rosé filled our empty bottles from the wine van's hose. A bundle of small violet-tipped artichokes to serve with fresh pasta in lemon butter. Pears and prunes and almond honey to make a tart."

On other days, three blocks of flowers continue down a wide tree-lined promenade. The area is brought to life with pots of bougainvillea, mimosa, stacks of rosemary, lavender with its roots packed in cardboard sleeves, grape vines, bay trees and bunches of the irresistible extra long pale peach tulips. To ensure there is something for everyone, an antique market or brocante lined both sides of the area. We bought a classic pewter wine bucket, old cherrywood rolling pin, a blue tea pot, silver ladle, and a linen nightgown with the monogram *AM*.

The wine van shows up at the market to fill up your gallon jugs.

Bottles of fruity, green olive oil circle the fountain in the *Place aux Herbes*, the heart of the market in Uzès.

BRAISED LEEKS IN CRÈME FRAÎCHE

This is a simple vegetable side-dish to serve beside a piece of chicken or fish that would benefit from a sauced accompaniment. Always stock up on leeks at a market.

INGREDIENTS
4 to 6 leeks (thin and tender rather than fat and woody)
1 cup herbal or vegetable broth
1/4 cup crème fraîche

METHOD
1. Cut the root off the white end of the leeks and remove all but 1" of the green stalk.
2. Rinse then split length-wise keeping layers intact.
3. Lay cut side down in a 8" shallow pan which can be covered.
4. Pour broth over the leeks. Bring to a simmer for 20 minutes. Salt if necessary.
5. Lift out carefully with a slotted spatula.
6. Boil down whatever liquid is left to about 1/4 cup.
7. Stir in the cream to make a smooth sauce.
8. Pour over the leeks if serving immediately, or return leeks to the sauce in the pan to re-heat gently when required.

March 2, 1969 AVIGNON

The monsoons dogging us on this van trip prevented any attempt to experience the markets of Nîmes as recalled above on later trips. After quickly photographing the Roman *Maison Carrée*, we drove on to Avignon. A short detour took us to the *Pont du Gard*. We could smell spring on the forest path that leads up to the panoramic open site, chosen by the Romans for this famed aqueduct in 2AD. Two massive arched levels rise 160 feet to span the River Gard. Along the top is a narrow stone channel which carried water from Uzès to Nîmes for over five hundred years. In 1969 we were allowed to walk the precariously narrow topmost level, connecting the two hills. We walked back on the first level which opens onto the river on each side and felt more secure for sightseeing.

If you are tempted to dance *Sur le Pont d'Avignon*, be careful not to fall off into the middle of the Rhone, because it only crosses the river halfway. The water was flowing full and fast as we stood staring down on the edge of this unfinished bridge. David had chosen a camp site on the banks of the Rhône for the night. He assured me that there would be enough caravans between us and the water. We woke up safely on Sunday morning and crossed the finished bridge to tour the Palace of the Popes, our shelter for the rest of the day. This former bishop's palace became a papal residence in the mid 1300s when the popes moved the papacy to avoid violent chaos in Rome. Their stay in Avignon ended in 1377 with a papal chism. Tours on a Sunday, complete with guide, are half-price. So for forty cents we happily wandered the halls of the papal palace, admiring the blue walls painted with songbirds in golden foliage.

The Avignon market had long tables of dried grains, spices and fruits which inspired an easy supper while recalling recent French history.

During the time that Algeria was a colony of France, the cultures and cuisines mixed with migration in both directions. Large bowls of couscous are prominent at street markets and take-aways, a great nutritious fast food. Limited space and equipment in our van kitchen made a grain fruit salad the choice, rather than the traditional couscous simmered on top of lamb stew.

The 2,000 year-old Pont du Gard still stands intact with its top channel ready to carry water from Uzès to Nîmes.

JEWEL COUSCOUS SALAD

Pre-cooked couscous makes this recipe a breeze. A variety of dried and fresh fruits and spices at the Avignon market suggested the title. At our local Canadian market one August, I found a pint of ground cherries, covered in a fine papery husk like a tomatillo. "I will include these in my couscous salad," I said to Rick, the farmer who had grown them. "Ah, you must be making a sweet couscous," he replied. It was the first time I had heard the distinction between sweet/savoury in this regard. Dried cherries can be substituted.

INGREDIENTS

1/2 cup pre-cooked couscous grains soaked in 1/2 cup boiling water
    with a pinch of salt

1/4 cup dried cranberries

1/4 cup dried apricots, diced

1/4 cup yellow raisins

1/4 cup husked ground cherries or dried cherries

2 dried figs, soaked in some warm water or apple juice to soften then
    diced

3 tablespoons lightly toasted pine nuts

2 tablespoons sliced green onions

2 teaspoons lemon juice

2 tablespoons olive oil

1 tablespoon chopped mint

1/4 teaspoon salt

1/8 teaspoon ground cumin

1/8 teaspoon ground coriander

METHOD

1. Soak the couscous grains in boiling salted water for 10 minutes. Fluff with a fork.
2. Toss in the fruits and nuts from the first section of ingredients.
3. Whisk the dressing ingredients together with the seasonings in the second group.
4. Pour over the bowl of salad and toss lightly.

This can be served with barbecued meats or small pita pockets stuffed with hummus.

March 3, 1969   ARLES

Three more days of unbroken rainfall hastened us along the road east, with only a very dim view of Arles in passing. The fabled light of Provence that drew Van Gogh out into the golden fields completely eluded us. Hours of confinement in the van, spent drawing designs for an imaginary kitchen store or making sketches of future advertisements, drove us out into the drizzle, draped in oilskins. Not even rain could rob the backstreets of Arles' old quarter of charm. To find a small *boulangerie* tucked under a Roman arch, and buy a monstrous warm *baguette*, which has to be stuffed under your raincoat for protection, is one of a shopper's delights in any small *provençal* town, no matter what the circumstances.

Two days each week, produce vendors and artisans line the *Boulevard des Lices*, an area that Arlesiénnes transform into an open-air stage for festivals during the year on special weekends. David sat at a café shaded by plane trees and watched me join the action. Butchers of Arles' sausages were especially proud of the ones made from *taureau sauvage*, bulls whose luck had run out in the Roman arènes. Spring lambs dangled from hooks around their stalls. A produce vendor encouraged me to buy a few small violet artichokes to eat raw, as a crudité with a crock of salt and one of olive oil for dipping. Several stalls displayed sacks of Camargue rice, considered the best delta grain.

This city on the Rhône River was a Greek settlement before the Romans made it their central Mediterranean hub, so I was drawn to the ageless products of both empires - onions, anchovies and olives - transformed by the baker's stall into a *pissaladière*.

Van Gogh lived above a café on this square, *Place du Forum*,
where he painted the starry *Night Café*.

A RIFF ON PISSALADIÈRE

If this were an authentic pissaladière, it would not include the tomatoes our neighbours had picked half an hour earlier. Traditionally, the Provençal version of pizza is made with onions, black olives and anchovies. I have taken liberties.

INGREDIENTS
2 small onions, peeled and finely chopped (1 cup)
2 cloves garlic, peeled and sliced
2 large Spanish onions, peeled and thinly sliced
2 tablespoons olive oil
1/4 teaspoon crumbled thyme leaves
sprinklings of salt and pepper
2 garden tomatoes, sliced thinly
12 pitted and halved black olives
6 anchovy fillets from a jar, preserved in oil
1 tablespoon olive oil
a nine inch pastry shell or thin pizza dough base
1 tablespoon granular mustard

METHOD
1. Preheat oven to 400F.
2. Sauté the chopped onions and garlic in olive oil over low heat until soft. Toss frequently to avoid browning. Set aside.
3. Add a little more oil to the pan if necessary to sweat the onion slices, thyme and seasonings over low heat for 30 minutes until they are translucent. Keep a close watch and adjust heat to prevent browning.

4. Baste the pastry shell with mustard and pre-bake for 10 minutes. It is not necessary to do this with a pre-made pizza dough.
5. Spread the chopped onion mix on the bottom. The sliced onions go over them evenly.
6. Arrange the anchovy slices like spokes on a wheel with the tomato slices in between and one in the centre. Scatter several olive halves in each section, saving one for on top of the tomato slice in the centre. Sprinkle lightly with seasonings and oil.
7. Bake for 20 to 30 minutes, depending on the type of dough used.

RICE AND SQUASH GRATIN

The Camargue delta, where the Rhone River empties into the Mediterranean, produces a reddish-brown short-grained rice, noted for its nutty flavour. As we drove beside the étangs between Languedoc and Provence, we tried a variety of local rice casseroles. We also stocked up on a fine sea salt produced on these marshes and herbs of Provence to flavour our cooking.

This would make a hearty supper for two or serve as a side dish at a table for four.

INGREDIENTS
1/2 cup risotto rice
1 small white onion
3 tablespoons olive oil (hold one in reserve)
1-1/4 cup vegetable broth
1 green and 1 yellow small round patty pan summer squash
sea salt to taste
pepper
1/2 cup chopped Italian parsley
1/2 cup grated Emmenthal cheese
1 large tomato

METHOD
1. Preheat the oven to 375 F.
2. Peel and chop the onion.
3. Warm 2 tablespoons of the oil in a large skillet. Sauté the onion until translucent but do not let it brown.

4. Heat the broth while you coat the rice grains with the onion and oil in the skillet.

5. Over medium-low heat, introduce the broth in stages, stirring frequently as for a risotto, allowing the rice to absorb the liquid before adding more.

6. Cut the small summer squash into quarters, then each piece into slices. Do not peel.

7. Lightly film another large skillet with oil. Stir fry the squash slices for about 4 to 5 minutes. These are so tender, they do not require much cooking.

8. In a bowl, incorporate the cooked rice and onion with the cheese and parsley.

9. Season to taste with sea salt.

10. Lightly oil a 9" oval au gratin dish. Spread the rice mixture evenly over the bottom. Sprinkle on a little water if the mixture seems too dry.

11. Lay the squash slices on top.

12. Place thin slices of tomato on top of the squash.

13. Sprinkle sparingly with sea salt and pepper.

14. Bake until heated through - about 15 to 20 minutes.

No paintings of Van Gogh remain in Arles, despite the fact that he lived in a room of *un café du nuit*, a place that stayed open all night, on the *Place du Forum* where he painted two remarkable canvases - Café Terrace at Night and The Night Café (1888). The interior scene in deep greens and reds, with a large billiard table in the centre, depicts a depressing scene of habituées, slumped over café tables, lounging the night away. His rented room was behind this dispirited bar.

We sat on the terrace of this café, which presents a much gayer exterior of bright yellow walls with door frames trimmed in electric blue, just as Van Gogh had painted it while seated outside at one of these small tables on a starry night. Rumour has it that he painted on the dark square with candles affixed around the wide brim of his straw hat. In his honour, we drank very strong espressos accompanied by several chocolate brandy truffles.

An auberge, near the entrance of the farm where our camp was located, was popular with local business men. We have the rotten weather to thank for driving us into *La Bergerie Provençale*, where we could have experienced one of the most memorable meals of our life but for our transitory bout of parsimony. We flung our wet selves into chairs nearest the fire to drip-dry. The fireplace was one of those French country magazine photo shots, all massive beams and stone. Gnarled tree roots were piled in the alcove at the side; blackened tongs and grills dangled around the opening. We were about to discover that attractive old kitchen implements were not merely decorative accents. A white oval platter, holding a raw, thick lamb cutlet, was warming on the hearth when we sat down. Soon the waiter took one of the pokers, raked up a bed of hot coals, placed a blackened grill on top of them, and threw on the cutlet. A wooden box, partitioned for salt and *herbs de provence*, hung beside the fireplace. A sprinkling from each section was added when the meat was turned. It was placed, sizzling onto a warmed dinner plate, and set before one of the local businessmen. We had ordered fishcakes, the lowest priced item on the menu. This ill-judged caution has caused a lifetime of regret. I cannot look at a lamb chop without thinking of that lucky man in Arles who taught us how to order like a businessman instead of like a student.

David had to turn away from the grilled lamb chops that he had not ordered.

March 5, 1969 MARSEILLE

Marseille the colourful, Marseille, the gay bustling port, remains a smear in our memory, obliterated by torrents lashing the windows of the van. *Il pleuvait* all the way there; *il pleuvait* as we parked in the municipal camping site; *il pleuvait* encore as we bussed into town for provisions. In the fifteen minutes that it didn't rain, we walked around the old harbour (the *Lacydon* of the Greeks) teeming with sailboats, fishing dories and luxurious yachts. In that short space of time, we could feel that this port was a rich melting pot of Arabs, Africans and Europeans, which had been brewing for 2500 years. Around the fish market here, another heady stew has been simmering for centuries - *la bouillabaisse*-whose praises have been sung by food notables like Julia Child and M.F.K. Fisher. Tradition and writers agree that the firm-fleshed fish specific to the area: rockfish, mullets, sea eels, bream, are necessary for the unique flavour and texture. But comparable seafood substitutes can be made, as long as the broth contains the basics of Mediterranean cuisine - olive oil, onions, garlic, tomatoes and saffron.

BOUILLABAISSE

Generally, bouillabaisse restaurants offer large bowls of white fish and crustaceans swimming around together in a rich tomato broth. The version prepared at Le Bacon, an elegant terrace on the water near Cap d'Antibes, impressed us by its simplicity and the manner in which it was served. Our waiter assured us that this was the authentic presentation.

A tureen of aromatic fish broth is placed on the table with a platter of white fish, a bowl of fiery rouille, plain boiled potatoes and crusty bread. Rosé from the area is served very cold.

Our fish monger in the Covent Garden Market rummaged in the back freezer and came up with a 3 pound bag of frozen cod meat chunks on the spinal skeleton. I set it to thaw in 2 inches of boiling water before beginning.

Fish for the stock or for the poached final pieces, can be chosen from the following regionally available species, fresh or frozen:
sea bass, cod, flounder, haddock, perch, pollock, red snapper, grouper, pickerel, turbot, hake.

Ingredients
For the fish stock:
1 medium cooking onion finely chopped
1 medium leek, white part with a little pale green, finely chopped
the above should come to about 2 cups in total
1/3 cup olive oil
2 large cloves of garlic chopped into eighths
1 cup chopped slices from a fresh fennel bulb
1 cup celery stalk and leaves mixed
1 cup freshly puréed tomatoes

The herbs included in this stock represent, in my mind, three aspects of the region:

1/4 cup chopped fresh basil

1/8 teaspoon fennel seeds

2 tablespoons ferny leaves from the fennel bulb

1/2 teaspoon fresh tarragon

Those four contribute the distictive anise flavour. Some cooks add a dash of Pernod to enhance this aspect.

1/3 cup chopped fresh flat-leaved parsley

leaves stripped from four sprigs of thyme

1 large bay leaf

The above three herbs are typically Mediterranean.

1/4 teaspoon cayenne

1/4 teaspoon saffron

These recall Moroccan flavours, popular around Marseille.

3 to 4 pounds fish bones, head, flesh from above list. No shellfish is included, but you can add -

1 cup bottled clam juice

1 tablespoon sea salt

6 grinds black pepper

six pieces of firm fleshed white fish - 2 each of three selections from the above list. My market choice was bass, haddock and yellow perch.

LA ROUILLE

2 egg yolks

1/2 cup olive oil

1/2 cup chopped red peppers which have been broiled then skinned (pimentos)

3 large garlic cloves minced

hot sauce

salt

METHOD

For the fish broth:

1. If your pieces of bone and bits for boiling are frozen, boil them in a few inches of water to thaw.
2. In a large stock pot, warm the oil and stir in the chopped onion and leek until they are coated and starting to soften.
3. Add the chopped celery, fennel bulb and garlic to the mixture in the pot. Sweat together in the warm oil over low heat until translucent (7 minutes max).
4. Stir in the tomato sauce.
5. Blend in all of the herbs.
6. Add the fish stock ingredients and water in which it thawed if available. You may remove excess skin and bones from meatier bits if possible. Pour on 6 cups of water and the clam juice if using. Stir in salt and pepper.
7. Simmer for 40 minutes tasting frequently to achieve correct amounts of seasonings.
8. Strain liquid into another pot through a large holed colander.
9. Remove bones, bay leaf and other large bits from the material in the colander. Put about one cup of the vegetable and soft flesh back into the broth. Purée with an immersion blender or through a food mill fitted with largest strainer holes. Add more solids if needed to thicken the broth to a coating consistency. Check seasoning balance. Add a pinch more cayenne if too bland.

LA ROUILLE

If you have a knack for it, you can whip up your own mayonnaise, otherwise use one half cup of good quality prepared mayo.

Using a blender or processor, whirl in:

2 large garlic cloves

pinch of saffron or 1/2 teaspoon paprika for colour

1/2 cup roasted and peeled red peppers or prepared pimentos from a
  jar

several drops of hot sauce, depending on strength and preference

1/4 teaspoon salt

ASSEMBLING :

1. Boil one medium potato or several smaller ones per person.

2. Bring soup to the boiling point. Put in whole fillets of your choice
   to poach two at a time.
   Lift out with a strainer to a warm platter when beginning to flake.

3. Drain and halve the potatoes when done. Arrange them around the
   fish on the platter. Sprinkle with parsley.

4. Place broth in a warmed tureen on the table with the platter of fish,
   a basket of crusty bread and a bowl of rouille.

5. A ladleful of broth is poured over a piece of fish and potatoes in each
   soup bowl. Each person takes a spoonful of rouille on the side if they
   wish.

If the campsite had been congenial, perhaps we would have waited out the rain to take in a few more of the sights. It was crammed with permanent trailers and the temporary home of a Paris circus troupe. In long barrack-like washrooms, bareback riders, smeared with grease paint, sauntered past in billowing mid-fifties crinolines. The lion tamer strutted between the caravans in high black boots, swishing his whip against the tires. Dogs snarled beneath the vans. Big Sister announcements kept coming over the public address system. A surfeit of local colour booted us out on to the road to Toulon.

As you stroll along the promenade of France's largest naval base, you are flanked by battleships on the starboard side, and souvenir stores on the port side. The scene had changed a lot from the early 1940's when this historic port had been captured by the Nazis and the French fleet scuttled their own ships (after some stern words from Winston Churchill), rather than have them fall to the use of the enemy. The original cobbled streets that had escaped the 1944 bombing, were lined with market stalls whose red and blue awnings set under a row of pollared plane trees added a much needed splash of colour to the brown stone buildings and still grey skies.

Our route from Toulon took us through fishing ports, such as Cassis, whose luminous light had inspired artists Roger Fry, Duncan Grant and Wyndam Lewis. A colony of British writers and artists came in the wake of Vanessa Bell and Virginia Woolf, who had brought their families and other Bloomsberries for holidays in the 1920s. *Much of our French culture began with gastronomic experience*, confessed Angelica Garnett, Vanessa's daughter in *The Charleston Magazine*. Virginia, frequently depressed by the gloom and darkness of England, found real happiness eating an omelette and quaffing the cheap but good wine, in the golden light of Cassis. In their book, Bloomsbury and France, Mary Ann Caws and Sarah Bird Wright tell us, "*It was France that prevented Bloomsberry from remaining insular.*"

And Cassis was the town that they returned to most often, at one point placing an offer to purchase a property. Leonard Woolf describes the town as extremely quiet, still dominated by the local people. When he returned there alone in 1951, the creeping development and increased traffic appalled him. In the sixties, we still considered it fairly unspoiled although he would probably have been disappointed. Memories of ideal times can often put paid to future enjoyment.

Driving through this part of the Riviera was like touring a long, continuous garden. Tropical growth overhung the road. Market gardens bulged with the tall peach and pink tulips that I had noticed stuffed by the dozens in the street market baskets of Toulon. In one of those quintessential vignettes that encapsulates cultural values, an elderly Frenchman rode a bicycle beside our van, a generous bunch of these tulips strapped onto the panier at the back. Scents floated down from unseen herbs on the hills surrounding us. This section of the countryside produced the over three hundred essences required to distill into one perfume. Luxury villas, surrounded by hedges of bougainvillea and jasmine, dotted the slope to the sea. Many of these had been built between the wars by a group of bright young socialites, a fun-loving generation that Gertrude Stein called lost. Perhaps lost to their conventional life styles; but they had found a place in the sun.

The heady scent of mimosa flooded our next campsite which had the lyrical name *Clair de Lune*. Now when I hear this piece of music by Ravel, the perfume and the setting return in full force. We walked in a mimosa-induced trance down the wet lanes of *Giens*, gathering bunches that had fallen over fences, to decorate the van that night back up at the campsite of moonlight. Overcome by the potent scent intensified by the moist air, at one in the morning, in a swoon, we had to toss the bouquet out the door.

March 7, 1969 HYÈRES

Hyères achieved fame as a health resort when Queen Victoria and other notables came to bathe in its waters. This French version of Bath still has all the amenities of a spa; water springs from fountains centred in the palm-lined avenues; large comfortable old hotels set the correct tone. We followed a snaking trail of food vendors' carts up medieval lanes, under stone archways, to emerge in the open *Place Massillon* in time for the excitement of the daily market. In this country, where food was entwined with culture, the daily markets were a celebration of this union. We stocked up on three days' worth of provisions from carts groaning under piles of the amazing bounty from land and sea. The stalls offered all the picnic essentials - cheeses wrapped in vine leaves, a chunk of smoked sausage rolled in black peppercorns, olives stuffed with garlic, plums and pears. A wise move, as our next stop lived up to its reputation for high prices.

March 8, 1969 ST-TROPEZ

Our arrival in St-Tropez was coincidental with the re-appearance of the sun. Now this really felt like the fabled Côte d'Azur. One dash into town where the international set were swanning around in cashmere and pearls, set me scurrying back to the van to unearth my Anne Klein suede suit and knee-high boots, the only camping ensemble that would cut the scene. We took our seats at the café on the harbour to sip brandy and Perrier with the best of them. David dug out his oil paints and easel, to follow in the steps of Paul Signac, Matisse and Bonnard, who had all painted this harbour. Granted, the fishing dories had been replaced by yachts, but the ochre and pink buildings lining the harbour were still there. He found it difficult to concentrate surrounded by an admiring group of femmes draped in silk.

St-Tropez's celebrity status was confirmed in 1956 when Brigitte Bardot and Roger Vadim shot the film, *And God Created Women*, linking the little fishing village with the hedonism of the movie world. While David daubed paint onto his canvas, I watched a film in the making on the long pier across the harbour. A girl in an orange dress stands in the front of a moving jeep, whose back seat is filled with balloons, points excitedly out at the boats while rumpling the driver's hair. Not a main feature. They ran through it gaily enough twice, then the jeep broke down. The girl in orange shivered for an hour or so on the pier. Up and running again, they went through the scene over a dozen times. Even Brigitte would have palled at this point. David finished his painting before the scene was in the can. It made us appreciative of the hard work behind the magic of the movies.

One afternoon we climbed the hill behind St-Tropez, up beyond the little clock tower, to the oddest cemetery of the trip. Suspended between a blue sea and a blue sky, white crosses floated among china wreath tributes, lilies, pansies and orchids, all blooming eternally on the hillside. When I had worked in a china store in the fifties, there was a vogue for these permanent bouquets of roses, finely sculpted then painted, to sit on coffee tables with only an occasional damp cloth to keep away the dust. This unique expression of floral tributes suggested that even in death the fashion-conscious of St-Tropez required chiselled perfection. They never wished to appear wilted.

The fact that Colette, France's most revered female writer lived here for a while, encouraged me to make a few inspired journal entries. I positioned myself on a canvas chair in the sun at the edge of the harbour and wrote a synopsis of our personal growth over the last eight months. If we were still in Windsor, I would be sitting behind a desk, marking spelling tests. Later, at the kitchen table in the breakfast nook, we'd check *Better Housekeeping* for a fast meal recommendation. It would be a cold night, but there might be a good movie on the boob tube about the south of France. In less than the nine months' normal gestation period, we had created different lives. I had the satisfaction of knowing on the eve of my twenty-eighth birthday, that I was starting to do what felt natural.

As we drove out of the playgound of the rich and famous, we noticed that the movie group had moved on to a scene where the girl jumps out of the jeep, and runs over to fetch two wine glasses perched on a stone wall. It may show up some time on late-night TV.

Ann waiting for a pick-up, harbourside, St-Tropez.

Luxury yachts face the dockside at Cannes, now dominated by the huge *Palais des Festivals.*

March 10, 1969   ST-RAPHAEL

St-Raphael was a perfect place to mark an occasion, my twenty-eighth birthday. The Art Nouveau buildings and palm-lined promenade help to maintain the romance of a Belle Epoque resort by the sea. For the birthday dinner we chose a small restaurant which seated eight couples near the harbour. The sixteen franc menu allowed us to order four courses: *soup aux poissons avec croutons et fromage; escargots en coquette; entrecôte saignant garni avec pommes frîtes et tomates grillés; tarte aux pommes.* Standard fare for a small French restaurant, but useful practice in proceeding through the ballet of a menu. Details of service intrigued us. The snails came in their own little partioned dishes with a great oil, parsley and garlic sauce. Under the watchful eye of the waiter, we passed the challenge of using escargot tongs properly. David's sketch of the escargot dish with the correct tongs and two-pronged fork, eventually appeared on a recipe card which we handed out with each purchase of this specialized equipment in our business. The apple tart was not a wedge cut from a round disc like mum's. Our servings were sliced from a long rectangle of puff pastry topped with thin slices of glazed apple. Now I found out how to handle a rectangular removable base flan tin. Proper presentation enhances the respect for the basic ingredients of a meal. The waiter's recommendation of a litre of local rosé reflected his wise assessment of our means and taste.

If you want to make a 1960s RETRO BIRTHDAY DINNER here are the recipes for the one served to us. The fish soup is optional.

ESCARGOTS

Decades ago, escargots appeared on every tourist menu tacked to the door of a bistro. Now they have sunk from sight, but not from memory. On a return trip a few years after this first taste, a plate of 12 fat, succulent snails in their shells were set before us with a chilled bottle of Chablis at a hotel in the town of the same name.

A tin of snails usually contains 24 in a brine. The natural shells can be purchased with the tin or with packaged frozen snails the first time you try them, but they are re-usable. Wash them out by filling a bowl of hot soapy water to soak them, then rinse.

INGREDIENTS

4 ounces unsalted butter
2 tablespoons olive oil
1/4 cup minced parsley
1/4 cup minced tarragon
2 cloves minced garlic
1/4 teaspoon salt
4 grinds of black pepper
1 small shallot or the white ends of 3 small green onions finely chopped
1 tablespoon cognac

METHOD
1. Blend all of the stuffing ingredients together in a processor.
2. Drain the escargots. Place 1/2 teaspoon of the blend in the bottom of each shell. Turn the snail in, corkscrew end first with flat end facing up. Fill with more butter stuffing.

3. Set each shell in the depression of special individual stainless steel or earthenware dishes. Since most people eat this rarely, an alternative to specialized plates is to hollow out a mushroom cap large enough to accommodate the butter sauce and the snail. Individual round au gratin dishes will also work.

4. If time allows, refrigerate several hours to allow the seasoning flavours to penetrate the snails.

5. Preheat the oven to 400F.

6. Place the four plates on a baking tray for ease of handling in the oven and to catch any spillage.

7. Bake for 10 minutes until the butter begins to bubble out.

8. Special tongs are needed to hold the hot shells while you skewer out the snail with small two-tined forks. But the best part is mopping up the seasoned hot garlic butter with slices of baguette.

9. Make sure the bottle of Chablis is well-chilled and the bread is warm.

STEAK/FRÎTES

This iconic bistro plat is seared in a heavy skillet so that a concentrated finishing sauce can be made by deglazing the pan. For two servings, we choose about 3/4 pound of rib-eye or cap, bone-in if available. The market butcher provides high-quality, organic meat, hormone free.

INGREDIENTS

3/4 to 1 pound marbled rib-eye or cap, cut 3/4 to 1 inch thick

1 tablespoon butter

1 tablespoon olive oil

1/4 cup red wine

2 tablespoons herbal butter (see page 241 of *Hungry Hearts*)

You may blend in 1 tablespoon chopped parsley or tarragon or thyme, according to taste.

salt and freshly ground pepper

METHOD

1. Melt the butter and oil together in a 10 inch cast iron fry pan.
2. Dry both sides of the steak and fry quickly over medium high heat, allowing 5 minutes each side for medium rare.
3. Transfer meat to a warmed platter to rest while preparing the sauce.
4. Pour off any excess oil remaining in the pan.
5. Pour in the wine and bring it to a rapid boil. If the platter contains any juices from the resting meat, dribble it into the pan. Use a wire whisk to scrape up and incorporate any crusted bits on the bottom.
6. When the liquid has reduced by half, swirl in the herbal butter, salt and pepper.

7. Dribble over meat before serving.

INGREDIENTS FOR FRITES
2 large oval Yukon Gold potatoes
1/4 cup olive oil
coarse salt

METHOD
1. Preheat oven to 400F.
2. Peel the potatoes. Cut into long 1/4 inch slices then into 1/4 batons.
3. Toss in a bowl with the oil to coat completely.
4. In the oven, warm a baking tray large enough to hold the fries in one layer with a little space separating them.
5. Use a wide spatula to turn them over after 10 minutes. Bake for another 10 minutes.
6. Sprinkle with salt before piling onto a plate beside the steak.

Beaujolais is traditionally poured to accompany this meal.

TARTE AUX POMMES

This is the most basic version of countless recipes for this standard dessert. It appears at its most elegant when baked and served from a 14" by 4" rectangular tin with a removable base.

INGREDIENTS

4 medium Granny Smith apples (good bakers)

juice of 1/2 a lemon

3 tablespoons granulated sugar (keep a vanilla bean in your jar of sugar)

2 tablespoons of unsalted butter

the same amount of pastry required for a standard 9" pie. Recipes for pastry are given on pages 211 to 212 of *Hungry Hearts*. Or use a section of frozen puff pastry from the store.

METHOD

1. Preheat oven to 400F.
2. Peel, quarter and core 4 medium apples. Slice each quarter lengthwise into approximately six thin slices.
3. Toss the slices in the juice from half a lemon to prevent discolouration
4. Lightly butter the tart tin. Roll out the pastry to fit and line the tin. Sprinkle the base with 1 tablespoon of sugar.
5. Closely overlap the apple slices down the length of the pan in two parallel lines.
6. Sprinkle with 1 tablespoon of sugar and dot at frequent intervals with small knobs of butter.
7. Use the remaining slices to form a third row of apples on top, down

the centre of the other two rows.

8. Sprinkle with 1 tablespoon of sugar and dot with butter.

9. Bake in the centre of the preheated oven for about 40 to 45 minutes until the pastry seems crisp and the apple edges are beginning to brown.

Our campsite, a few kilometres past St-Raphael, was built on terraces, similar to that first one in Spain. From our ledge we looked out through bushes of yellow mimosa towards a sailboat drifting in a moonlit bay. When we reached the pebbled beach on our way out of town in the morning, a sign indicated that on August 14, 1944, the American 36th infantry landed here to begin the push up through Austria into Germany. We drove through the fishing village of Villefranche-sur-Mer, where the American fleet had docked for years in its deep harbour. The merchants welcomed the sailors and the women married them. We returned here on our thirtieth wedding anniversary.

VILLEFRANCHE-SUR-MER
June 29, 1991

Several months before our thirtieth anniversary, I spotted a magazine photo-spread on Jean Cocteau's, *La Chapelle Saint Pierre*, situated on the bay of Villefranche-sur-Mer, one of the few villages along the Côte d'Azur where you can still watch small fishing boats go out and return with a catch. In 1925, Cocteau sat on a balcony of the Hotel Welcome watching the parade of sailors, artists and lost generationists who paraded the seafront. But most of all, he stared at the abandoned chapel across the street where the fishermen stored their nets. He returned in the 1950s to restore and decorate this old chapel with magical murals and imagery depicting the life of Peter, the fisherman/apostle, walking among the gypsies and locals of the village.

We decided to book a room in the Hotel Welcome facing this chapel for the June week when we were married years ago. As I sat in the warm sun on "Cocteau's" little balcony, enjoying his scene of seventy years earlier, David set a *petit dejeuner* tray on my lap - jugs of coffee, warm milk and a croissant with a pink diamond ring buried in its buttery folds. Good thing I was eating slowly. And the rest of the day got even better. The priest held a blessing for the fishermen in Cocteau's chapel. A bride, in white gown and veil, sailed out of the harbour on a yacht. A brass band paraded under our window to herald the start of *the festival of flowers*. Townsfolk and tourists lined the harbour pelting the small craft in the water with armloads of lilies, tulips, daisies and carnations to ensure another year of bountiful fishing. Only one thing was wrong with this ideal week. We had stayed in a hotel rather than a house with a kitchen, where I could prepare the daily catch and set those flowers in a vase on the table.

A room with a view of the deep naval harbour at Villefranche.

Flash Forward

VILLEFRANCHE REVISITED
March 2006

After our forty-fifth anniversary, I decide it is time to re-do Ville-franche, only this time more like a native. For weeks I trawl the web for a suitable vacation rental, until I spot an apartment with hot scarlet gera-niums, suspended in terra cotta planters from an ornate iron balcony over a brilliant blue sea. Long french windows connect this small bal-cony to a modern Italian kitchen on the top floor of a faded pink three-storey nineteenth century house on the *Basse Corniche* running above Villefranche. These generous seven-foot glass rectangles are repeated along the livingroom and bedroom wall, bringing a Matisse mural of palm trees and white sails floating on an indigo sea into our temporary home. Our bed juts out over the Med. Swallows brush the fronds as they flash across the windows. I put on sun glasses indoors to soften the sparkle of bright rays bouncing on the whitecaps. Matisse's enthusiasm suddenly makes sense: *"Luminosity of light....When I realized I would see that light every morning, I could not believe my happiness."*

From my perch in a rattan armchair, I look right to see St Pierre's Chapel, still anchoring the harbour, near the fisherman's stall. After the fall of the Roman Empire, first Goths then Saracens raided this coast. The fishermen of Villefranche fled up to Mount Olivio above the vil-lage, and housing continues to cling to cliffs high up beyond the Grand Corniche. We follow a winding road, Montolivo, down to the present port that thrives on cruise ships ferrying in passengers for lunch at one of the many restaurants lining the quay. The pastel-hued houses rise in layers of ochre and peach with aqua and lime shutters under red tile roofs. An alternative route down, two hundred and fifty-seven steps cut into the side of the hill, descends beneath arcs of pink bougainvillea and wisteria, passes terraced gardens of roses and freesias ending at a circle of necessary shops, newsagent, butcher, patisserie, green grocer, épicerie, ranged around café tables set under a tree.

Behind the blond wood cabinetry of this efficient kitchen, there are all the utensils and cookware we need to experiment with the cuisine of the area. A phrase used to describe the life-style of the coast, *fait niente*, works for our approach to the food. Ingredients are so fresh and flavourful that we literally do nothing to prepare it. We are here in March, the month to celebrate tastings from the first pressing of the olives. The olive stall, in a row of food vendors that line the municipal park on Saturdays, offers perfect small niçoise and an interesting mixture of black and green ones in herbs and oil. They also sell large bags of mixed herbs for specific dishes - fennel seeds, bay leaves and parsley - for fish.

"April is Fish Month", David reads from a local magazine, as he watches the small boat come into the harbour below us. "If you head down those two hundred and fifty-seven steps pronto, you just might get something for dinner." Perhaps he'll have the costly favourite of local restaurants, the loup de mer. I stand in line behind two Italian women, who are excited about buying slices of what looks like shark, but could be something else. I ask them if they bake it in the oven or grill it. "No. Un poco olio, in a pan avec ail et un soupçon de vin blanc". A recipe is cobbled together haltingly in three languages. "Cook quickly. *Pas plus que huit minutes.*"

On the hill road back up, a small green grocer displays some exquisite fraises de France, laid tenderly on fernery in a wicker basket. *Pas Espagnol, Madame. Ces francaises*, he explains with pride. I scoop up six of them, a tiny sweet Charentais melon, two artichokes to accompany the fish. See what I mean about easy but good? No wonder human life has been on this shore for four hundred thousand years. It still sustains life in all its abundance.

At midnight, I look left out of the panoramic windows to see all four glittering decks of a cruise ship disappear behind the promontory of St. Jean Cap Ferrat. A crescent silver moon floats with me over this spit of land, where the ghosts of Somerset Maugham, T.S.Eliot, Aldous Huxley and Noel Coward hover above the current villas of rock legends, Bono and Tina Turner. In daylight, we walk the curve of beach that will bring us to their gates. Train lines pass above us connecting with Monaco, Menton, and on into Italy. Trains we never boarded. Writer, Pierre Mac Orlan, coined the term *passive adventuring* to describe the appreciation of stillness in a world obsessed with movement. The scene framed in the windows beside this kitchen chair, connects me with a lifetime of imaginary travel adventures along the entire stretch of the Riviera.

If sitting passively is not your choice, a bus stops just under the kitchen window, that will carry you to *Juan le Pins*, the physical world of the Fitzgeralds.

Small fishing boats still go out to sea each morning from the dockside.

The catch is cleaned and sold on the spot.

March 12, 1969   NICE

On the drive along the coast, I was reading E.F. Benson's *A Breath of French Air*, not challenging reading, but bearing a title that did perfectly describe Nice. Gardens gay with beds of royal blue, rich magenta, purple and crimson blossoms blazed down the centre of the boulevards, no shrinking violets for this town. Bracing sea breezes whipped the tricolours on the lamp standards and lifted skirts. With a spring in our steps, we walked the expansive *Promenade des Anglais*, named for the nineteenth century English who funded the construction of this broad walk bordering the sea.

On that brisk March day in 1969, our youth combined with the openness, air and light to buoy our spirits and spur us to walk under the long batallion of palms with a vengeance. The waterfront wore a necklace of white luxury hotels, sparkling like a dowager duchess' diamonds in the sun. In spite of a liberty in the air that permitted topless bathers, the scene called to mind a Victorian fashion print, the ladies in crinolines and Paisley shawls, twirling parasols as they strolled with one hand on an escort's arm.

I waited in the van on the Promenade while David went to find the American Express office to pick up our mail. An hour slipped by like a few minutes in such a beautiful spot while David found his way out of the narrow streets of *le vieux ville*. The sea is easy enough to find except when you are entranced by the wonders of the old town.

This infectious sense of abandonment influenced our reception of the pile of letters waiting at the American Express office. News of student sit-ins at the University of Windsor; Mad March Hare neighbourhood parties; painting, wallpapering, planting and other nesting activities, made us even more appreciative of our bohemian existence. We were always anxious to receive letters from family and friends, and equally relieved to be out of the loop once we had read them. We regretted leaving Nice after just one day, but were eager to cross into Italy. But you don't have to leave so fast. The city made such a good impression, we have returned to Nice at least seven times since that first day and can offer the reader a fuller picture.

A vigorous stroll along the *Promenade des Anglais*, Nice.

NICE
March, 2009

LA VILLE EST LA VIE
THE CITY IS LIFE

Thanks to web magic, we located an apartment in an eighteenth-century block, in the historic centre of Nice, surrounded by all that gives value to life. From another wicker armchair beside another long window overlooking the flower market, I stare at Mount Boron, the ancient archeological headland where paleolithic man lit the first fires for cooking and comfort on these Mediterranean shores. Directly facing me is the tall yellow house where Matisse captured the light and life of this coast. Just below it, Greek sailors pulled their boats into the small bay and christened their new colony *Nikaia* in 400 BC. Centuries later, Isadora Duncan danced in one of the fishermen's huts she had converted into a studio. Our precariously small balcony hangs over *Cours Saleya*, four long rows of vendors' stalls loaded with olives and lavender from the hills that hug the bay and with glistening fish from its waters. Jewel-toned fruits and vegetables from Spain and Africa fill baskets under striped awnings that run parallel to palms fringing the Mediterranean.

At street level, four floors directly below us, *La Cave Bianchi*, has been supplying clients with vintage wines since 1860. On our first outing, David goes into this emporium where crystal chandeliers hang over wooden barrels, and is greeted by the owner, Frank Obadia, who gives him a tour of the cave and allows him to hold a 1961 St. Emilion. Mr Obadia is an artist who has painted wine signs and posters. He calls his exhibitions, *Wine-Man-Show*. During our six-week stay, we develop a preference for the pale rosés of Provence, particularly those from the Var

District out past the aeroport.

A professionally stocked kitchen store is next to our heavy green entry door. Rented kitchens always need a rubber spatula, a wooden spoon and an extra knife. At one corner of our block, Queen Victoria's stationary supplier is still in business. The Queen spent her last few winters in Nice and sent the staff down to our block to pick up some pens and ink. David went in often for watercolour brushes and painting pads. The gold leaf lettering of the Royal emblem has survived over their door and the business still remains in the Rontani family.

Across from this store is *Hotel de Ville*, Nice's City Hall. Under Napoleonic Code, all marriages must take place here in a civil ceremony. So every Saturday afternoon, a parade of honking cars circle our block on their way one street south to the grand *Promenade des Anglais* for miles of celebratory driving along the coast. The wedding parties pass the ornate Opera House that commands the block between us and the sea. Two doors along I am buying a bright yellow tin of oil at Alizari's, a family renowned for the olives grown on their lands. Across the street, in a gilt and glass 1850s decor, Confisserie Auer displays giant chocolate eggs and myriad boxes of pastel bonbons, tied with satin ribbons for Easter.

St-Francois-de-Paule has been at the heart of our block since 1773. Its square bell tower is visible from all parts of Nice. We use it as a signpost for the apartment when we are wandering around the city. As the sun sets, we sip campari and tonic opposite the Dominicans' small terrace garden. Our bedroom is just metres away from the two huge lead bells that make the room vibrate with joyous pealing.

The location's icing on the cake is *Bar de la Terrasse*, the small brasserie that anchors the key corner of the block. Every morning, steps from our front door, their chalkboard straddles the sidewalk announcing the chef's daily special plate. Our first day we slide onto the leather banquette facing the bar and order *quaille et potat rosti*. Each subsequent day, I check the board on my morning baguette run and schedule our activities accordingly. If the *plat du jour* sounds irresistable we visit a museum or a park in Nice rather than do a Riviera day trip. I start to keep a list of their plats in a notebook. The repertoire is extensive, with few repetitions during our stay and is all produced and served by a three-man team. The chef works from a six-foot square area, open to view at the end of the bar. The bartender fills the carafes with very reasonable house red, white or rosé, uncorks the name vintages, and pulls a serious espresso. The waiter deftly serves all twenty places as well as the few tables outside under the awning. One round table inside is reserved for a large bouquet of fresh blossoms.

On our return visit for *la tranche de gigot d'agneau aux herbs provençal*, the waiter brings us a complimentary liqueur glass of limoncello after we mop up every spot of the sauce with our bread. He realizes we are neighbours and offers *emportez* - we can take-away meals up to our apartment. No longer necessary to stay in town for the *plat du jour*. Once when David takes a train ride up into the mountains, I stay at home, shopping for vintage clothing in the flea market until it is time for lunch - *daube niçoise avec gnocchi*. Chunks of beef that fall apart on the fork in a dark, spicy sauce with a hint of orange, so good I asked for a take-away for David. While the waiter brings me a complimentary espresso, the chef scrapes all that is left of the day's special into a large white bowl for me to carry upstairs. The bartender willingly writes the name of the cut of beef used on the back of my bill where I jot down the other recipe ingredients.

This corner is close to the law courts, guaranteeing a steady clientele for their *lapin aux chausseurs spagetti* or *picatta de veau au citron*. But it is the quality of the ingredients and skill of the chef that brings back customers. Plus the fact that the plats range from 9 euros to 11 euros; there is no waiting, no attitude, no risk of disappointment.

Since coming home, we have attended a talk given by the urban designer for our city of London, Ontario. The phrases he used to describe a downtown that works were - "wholesome mix of commercial, residential, retail; variety dependent on density; improving design of apartment buildings; invest in attractive public spaces; pedestrian friendly." Some places never lost it.

Nice was actually an Italian town until 1860 and that cultural mix is evident in the pastel architecture and in the cuisine of the area. The flower and vegetable market offered every hue of olives; stalls sold slices of pissaladière, the southern French version of pizza, a savoury blend of onions, olives and anchovies on a tomato-smeared pastry crust. Ratatouille, that versatile vegetable stew that screams summer, still continues to influence our choice of plants for the garden. We try to grow eggplants, zucchini, tomatoes and peppers so that David can try a new variation on the *rata* theme every year. He currently favours roasting the vegetables first. Several Canadian cookery collections have asked permission to include his version of this provençal classic. My favourite from the area is the simpler *salade Niçoise*, with its chunks of tuna, eggs and those tiny black olives. A meal of pasta squares filled with puréed squash eaten our last evening in the old quarter of Nice, primed us for Italy.

Cours Saleya, a street through the centre of the old town, is filled with flower stalls in front of flat-roofed former fishermen's houses.

SALADE NIÇOISE

In his cookbook, Cuisine Niçoise, the controversial long-time mayor of Nice, Jacques Médecin, begs us never,never, to put boiled potatoes, or any other boiled vegetable, into a genuine salade Niçoise. I will obey him to a point - quickly blanched fresh beans are a component I feel should be included. I prefer to plate each serving individually, so that the salad is presented looking like a painting of the region, which it is. The following would compose four servings.

INGREDIENTS
12 large leaves of Romaine lettuce, washed and dried
1 small tin of tuna packed in oil
1 teaspoon capers
4 local field tomatoes (this salad should not be made in winter)
4 fresh basil leaves
2 hard boiled eggs
4 anchovy fillets
1/2 cucumber
1/2 pound of thin green and yellow string beans mixed
2 ounces tiny black Niçoise olives
4 tablespoons olive oil

METHOD
1. Line the plates with 3 leaves of Romaine each.
2. Mix the capers into the tuna. Place a rounded mound in the centre of each plate where the lettuce leaves meet.
3. Quarter the tomatoes. Arrange four quarters around each mound

of tuna.

4. Drape a basil leaf on each tomato.
5. Set one half of the boiled eggs on each plate. Lay an anchovy fillet over the yolk.
6. Peel and slice the cucumber. Arrange slices opposite each egg.
7. Top and tail the beans then blanch a few minutes in boiling salted water.
8. Pile about 8 of the drained beans opposite the cucumbers on each plate. You may have some left over.
9. Scatter the black olives.
10. If you do not like the thought of a bare anchovy, leave them off the eggs but try chopping one into the olive oil in place of salt. Mayor Médecin urges us to use only oil and salt as a dressing over this salad. No vinaigrette.

March 14, 1969 MONACO

We were relieved that the border was not far along the road, for we were down to our last twenty francs. And we still had to get through Monaco, city of high rollers. A mass of highrise buildings is crammed into an area smaller than New York's Central Park. The *Moyenne Corniche*. the highway above the city, afforded a spectacular free panorama of the oldest fairytale kingdom in the world. The Grimaldis have been monarchs here since 1297, and Princess Grace has insured that the line will continue for at least another generation. The turreted palace, with its guards in striped boxes, overlooks an azure bay, where luxury yachts bob beside the Olympic swimming pool. Black horse-drawn carriages with the royal crest painted on the doors, wait at the entrance to carry the Prince and Princess to a ball at the Casino, a lavish *Belle Epoque* building, designed by Charles Garnier, architect of the Paris Opera House. I would like to stand in the rain to see Princess Grace and Sophia Loren arrive resplendent, but David opts for taking the Corniche road to Italy. There goes our chance to double our last twenty francs with a throw of the dice. Instead, I went into a fine pâtisserie and bought two scrumptious cream-filled napoléons to eat by the roadside before we set off to drive through Menton, the last French city on the coastal road.

In spite of the fact that I did not buy kitchenwares in France, this country taught me to admire not only the form, but the function of beautiful cookware. When the author, Elliott Paul lived in Paris, a hardware store on his block rented out a large copper cauldron in which French housewives could prepare their preserves. He thought it was so beautiful he rented it for two months just to sit on a table in his attic room. The store owner considered this folly, another proof that Americans were crazy. Good cookware should be used for its intended purpose. He told him the preserving kettle would be even more beautiful full of cherries bubbling in a sugar syrup.

During our hurried stay in France, we visited street markets rather than museums, churches or galleries. In her booklet, *Pageants and Picnics*, Elizabeth David tells us that food markets should be considered part of a country's artistic traditions.

The Olympic swimming pool faces the route of
the Monte-Carlo Grand Prix.

ITALY
Poetry and Pasta

March 14, 1969   VENTIMIGLIA to ALASSIO

The fuel consumption needle indicated that we were at the end of the reserve tank as we cruised up to the Italian border. With only a few more yards of France to cross, we were loath to cash another cheque into francs in the days before widespread use of credit cards at gasoline stations. As we sat in the long line-up of cars waiting to cross the border, a hitch-hiker we had passed a few miles back drifted up to the passenger window.

"Your rear tire is flat lady." He almost seemed pleased. Of course it was pouring again, so I held the umbrella over David while he changed the tire. Our first stop in Italy was a gas station in Ventimiglia, an appropriate enough introduction to a country that was having a love affair with anything on wheels. In these dispiriting circumstances I took stock of the past few months. Spain and France with their wine, olives and sunshine had effectively closed the poetry books. St.Tropez had not seemed like the place to be reading Milton. Maybe Italy would rekindle that interest.

That first night in Italy, we slept in an empty campsite near Alassio, on a terraced hill overlooking an island in a small bay of the Ligurian Sea. To mark this introduction to the Italian Riviera, we found ourselves turning back to the poetry books. It couldn't be helped. *Italia* had been the home of Byron, Keats, Shelley and the Brownings for many years. It had nourished them with the inspiration for some of their greatest poetry and then had wrapped them in death. I understand the attraction. Coming into Italy always feels like returning home. Not because western civilization originated in the forums of the Caesars, but because the people seem so comfortable in their skins. Whether it's a bent signora scrubbing down a sidewalk, or a golden goddess with silk-draped legs flung over the side of a motorbike, they are at ease with themselves in the moment, the place where poetry happens. They seemed to be everything we were not; although we were more or less awash in verse that spring of 1969, our lives lacked poetic intensity. As we stared through the rain-streaked window of the van, we decided to get out our books and let the poets lead us across the top of Italy to the Adriatic coast.

March 15, 1969   GENOA

Genoa, the birthplace of Christopher Columbus, admired by Charles Dickens, probably merited a stop. But since every one of the campsites nearby was closed, all we remember of Genoa is an industrialized seaport under glowering skies blurred by the swish of windshield wipers. This city was designated as the European Capital of Culture for 2004, and is noted for its Genoese basil - great for making pesto. We will honour today's city with a culinary classic.

PASTA BAKED WITH CHEESE AND GENOVESE BASIL

The basil grown around Genoa is sweet, spicy and aromatic. Our large-leafed lettuce basil comes close. In this recipe, I make a simple version of pesto to spread on the pasta in the baking dish.

INGREDIENTS
1 cup shredded basil leaves
1 large garlic clove, peeled and sliced
1 tablespoon olive oil
1/2 cup grated Parmigiano-Reggiano
salt and pepper to taste

1 tablespoon olive oil
1 large clove of garlic, peeled and crushed
1/4 cup shredded basil leaves
2 cups (preferably home-made) tomato sauce

1/2 cup cubed mozzarella cheese
1/2 cup cubed fontina cheese
butter for coating baking dish

1-1/2 cup dried penne or rigatoni
salt

METHOD

1. Preheat oven to 350F.
2. Blend the first group of ingredients in a food processor or grind in a mortar and pestle.
3. Warm the garlic in the other tablespoon of oil. Stir in the 1/4 cup of fresh basil.
4. Add the tomato sauce and simmer for 15 minutes.
5. Boil the pasta in salted water until almost tender.
6. Butter a 9" by 12" baking dish.
7. Drain the pasta and toss it in with the tomato sauce.
8. Spread a layer of half the pasta over the baker.
9. Dot it with half of the pesto.
10. Distribute the cubed fontina cheese.
11. Repeat the layers finishing with the cubed mozzarella.
12. Bake in preheated oven for 20 minutes until cheese bubbles.

The next stretch of road could not be driven on a rainy night. The Automobile Association map describes the Bracco Pass as "a tedious two lane highway with gradients of one in seven. Overtaking impossible because of heavy traffic." Desperate to stay the night, we pulled in past a chioso sign to get some information from a workman.

"The weather is no cooler here than it was in Spain or France. Why are there not more campsites open?" It was answered by our first Italian shrug, accompanied by slightly different hand movements from the French shrugs. Then he waved us over to a spot under a tree with a view of the sea, hosed down our own private washroom, and bid us *buon giorno.*

The morning drive verified that overtaking on the pass is impractical but not impossible. We did manage to squeeze past several labouring transports on the tight twists up this gruelling road. The risks were offset by grand glimpses of the sea between the rugged peaks of the Ligurian Alps.

If the scarcity of open campsites concerned us, the poor conditions of those that were open was even more worrisome. The luxuries of Spanish and French facilities - hot showers, grocery stores, communal kitchens - had spoiled us. Just before *La Spezia,* we found ourselves alone in a muddy field with some chickens and a large black dog. It was as though the shore had been infected by a blight causing patches of decay that spread down to Livorno (Leghorn). Beaches were either dull, commercial or vulgar, with peeling pink change huts emblazoned with grand names, *Florida, Eden, Roma,* alongside the Coca Cola signs. The stretch of beach near *Marina di Masa* where we pitched camp, was particularly seedy. Garbage and cheap restaurants littered the bay from one end to the other. We had refused to stay in two other places, virtual mudholes that were asking more per night than the Spanish Benidorm campsite.

March 16, 1969   LA SPEZIA

David viewed this sad landscape as a personal insult to his favourite poet:

"Poor Shelley would drown himself again willingly if he could see how squalid parts of this coast have become" he moaned. From a castle at *Lerici* on this section of the coast, in July of 1822, he had set sail in his small boat, the *Ariel*, to visit friends. In his pocket was a copy of verses from *Adonais*, the elegy he had penned on hearing of Keat's death in Rome. It contained the lines:

> *From the contagion of the world's slow stain*
> *He is secure.*

The *Ariel* was caught in a Mediterranean storm, which washed Shelley's body ashore a week later. Ironically, it was buried in quicklime and sand, as the authorities, fearing an outbreak of plague, did not want him to "pollute" the beach. Lord Byron and Leigh Hunt burned it some time later to quell any further fears. Shelley's hopes for a world made beautiful by the enlightened rule of imaginative legislators lie buried with him near Keats in the Protestant Cemetery in Rome. The Italian Riviera has improved its image in the past forty years, but I'm not sure that even now it's what the Romantic poets had in mind.

March 17, 1969   PISA

We decided to take the autostrada direct to Florence, but were diverted by a camp just outside of Pisa, clean, comfortable, and free since it was not "officially" open. More importantly, our spirits received a much-needed lift from the quirky leaning tower that was within walking distance. Once through the thick stone walls of the city, a trio of remarkable buildings sit dramatically in the centre of a green park. The almost toppled tower, guaranteed to bring a smile to any face, is the *Campanile* or Bell Tower which actually holds seven bells. It began to sink before it was finished in 1173, due to a foundation only three metres deep set in unstable sub-soil. It was allowed to settle for a century before the builders had another go at it, this time constructing one side of each level taller than the other and attaching lead weights. The tilt increased. Recent adjustments have corrected the degree slightly so that it is now straighter than it has been in centuries.We could climb 296 steps to the top for a panoramic view of Pisa and the River Arno.

The other buildings in this grouping include the round, white stone Baptistry, shaped like the papal crown, dedicated to St. John the Baptist, and the solemn *Duomo of Santa Maria Assunta*. Mercifully, they had been given breathing space in this *Piazza dei Miracoli*. It really was a miracle that the ubiquitous souvenir stalls did not encroach on this classic scene. They were inconspicuous, banished to the other side of a wide boulevard, against a wall.

The white stone Baptistry, the *Duomo of Santa Maria Assunta* and the tipsy *Campanile* form an impressive grouping on the grassy *Piazza dei Miracoli* in Pisa.

The leaning tower is the straightest it has been since construction began in 1173.

March 18, 1969   FLORENCE

We entered *Firenze*, birthplace of the Renaissance, from the west, but our guidebook indicated that the municipal campsite was on the eastern side of the city. Even the most hardened philistine could not have remained unaffected by the barrage of art we encountered in that drive across Florence, "the Athens of the Middle Ages". Because art has been fused to the commercial life of the city since the days of the Renaissance artist/craftsmen, it impacts on every level, from museums to market stalls. It permeates small craft shops down dusky alleys, infiltrates trattorias and bars, shines from the goldsmiths' windows on the *Ponte Vecchio* and soars above the city in the red-tiled dome of the great *Duomo*. So I should not have been surprised that the municipal campgrounds were actually beautiful. But after a succession of dismal overnights, this was indeed a treat. High on a hill within the city limits, we parked amidst cypress trees and wild spring flowers. The pathway down to the hot showers was very romantic, ivy curled over the edges of old slabs of stones and the way was dotted with pieces of ancient chipped statuary, fragments of columns. A fountain niched into an old stone wall dripped with greenery. The grocery store sold *grappa*.

The standard Self-Service Cafeteria that we found in the town, was more of an art gallery than a restaurant. Every square foot of wall space in its several rooms, and even the square pillars that ran down the centre to support the roof, were panelled with oils, watercolours, prints, woodcarvings and bas-reliefs, all professionally framed. This creative onslaught stimulated table conversation. With the lasagna, we discussed the Renaissance; the veal moved us along to Impressionism; coffee and dessert inspired talk of Cubism. If we ate here often enough, we might actually become art critics.

View of the birthplace of the Renaissance from the *Piazzale Michelangelo*.

The corridor connecting the Uffizzi Gallery on the right bank of the Arno with the Pitti Palace on the left bank runs along the top of the *Ponte Vecchio*.

ART-INSPIRED VEGETABLE SIDE DISH

This simple accompaniment to a grilled piece of chicken or meat, is composed of the colours of the Italian flag, as are many other Italian dishes.

INGREDIENTS

for two servings - double the ingredients for four persons

4 pale, elongated (about 5") thin eggplants

salt

olive oil

2 large plum tomatoes, each sliced lengthways into four long slices

6 large basil leaves

4 thin slices mozzarella

METHOD

1. Preheat oven to 350F.
2. Slice each eggplant lengthways into three strips. Sprinkle with salt. Lay them on paper towelling for 15 minutes to draw out moisture. Pat dry.
3. Brush each slice lightly with oil and broil a few minutes per side.
4. Oil two individual 4" by 6" bakers or one large baker.
5. Line base with eggplant slices. Lay tomatoes on top. Sprinkle lightly with salt. Cover with basil leaves. Finish with cheese slices.
6. Bake in preheated oven for 15 minutes.

The city offered too many other enticing luncheon venues for us to be faithful to our first. One morning we trudged up a steep stone stairway, marked by the stations of the cross, to reach the *Piazzale Michelangelo* and the panoramic view down to all the bridges over the Arno. Every one of them had been rebuilt since the Second World War, with the exception of the Ponte Vecchio, which thankfully had been spared by a German general. Red-tiled rooftops stretch toward the dark green hills surrounding the city with villas nestled amongst firs and poplars. As we munched asiago and salami panini on the low stone parapets, we discussed the importance of aesthetics as a civic amenity. A half litre of Chianti and some fresh apricots transformed us into experts in town planning.

Our primary reason for visiting the Medici Library was to see the rows of walnut pews holding rare manuscripts on their slanted reading ledges. I would have preferred to see the room complete as it once was with scholar monks pouring over the original Greek and Latin treatises. One of them appeared and invited us to have our picnic lunch overlooking their peaceful courtyard. The sun warmed the spot we had chosen between the pillars of the cloister which overlooked the dome of the Duomo and Giotto's marble campanile rising above a sea of brick-coloured roofs. From this vantage point, monastic life seemed appealing.

The municipality had thoughtfully positioned a string of small grocery stores up on the hill adjacent to the camp grounds. On a daily basis, I made the rounds of the cheery merchants behind the counters of the meat shop, chicken shop, bread shop, milk shop, fruit and veg shop, and the anything-you-might-have-forgotten-shop. We did not discover the historic market building of Florence until ten years later when we rented a farmhouse in the Chianti hills. This little nucleus suited us just fine at this juncture and I found a chocolate sponge cake there one afternoon to share with Ted and Pam, the Canadians we had met in Spain, who had rejoined the caravan. Late that night in a fuggy van, four Canadian exiles discussed travel plans, our nebulous futures, and the beauty of Florence, over cups of cocoa laced with Italian brandy.

The third week of March, stimulated to a spending spree by the range of shopping venues in this city, we boldly cashed $100 travellers' cheques instead of the usual $50 allowance per week. I coveted the elegant leather accessories sported by the Florentines and a specific dress in the window of a toney boutique on the *Ponte Vecchio*. It was black silk, splashed with vivid long-stemmed red tulips and brilliant yellow daffodils. When I got up the courage to go in and ask the price, a quick calculation told me that this purchase would wipe out the rest of our travel horde. My growing appreciation of the finer things whispered that it might just be worth it, but David would probably tire of watching me wear our trip on my back. That left the leather goods. After window-shopping every shoe store along the back streets, I became the proud owner of a pair of brown leather pumps and a purse so soft I wanted to stroke it as we walked. I have it still in my closet.

Comfortably settled, I set us a rigourous sightseeing schedule for the next day — a tour of the vast *Palazzo Pitti* in the morning, followed by a visit to the fifteenth century *Palazzo Guidi*, where Elizabeth Barrett had found shelter with Robert Browning after fleeing from her tyrannical English father. "Best not to wear those new shoes." David was referring to the beautiful soft brown leather pumps that I had bought in an attempt to appear Italian. Three hours later, having ignored his advice and tramped the miles of marble in the Pitti, I hobbled up to the massive doors of the *Palazzo Guidi* clutching the brown bag and my injured pride. Elizabeth christened their suite of rooms within the palazzo, *Casa Guidi*, to add a coziness to the only home they would ever share. I tried to imagine these rooms behind the elegant arch of grey stone where she had written her *Sonnets from the Portuguese*, borne their son, Pen, and died, content with the new life she had found in Italy. Her husband's verse,

Open my heart and you will see,
Graved inside it, Italy.

is engraved on the walls of their son's palazzo on the Grand Canal where Robert returned to die.

I pulled open the massive doors, eager to enter their love story. Inside *Casa Guidi* there were several apartments with a sign indicating that the historic one was up a flight of stone steps. On the Brownings' door another sign informed the visitor that the hour of opening was four p.m. Since it was only two p.m. and my feet were throbbing, I had to be satisfied with a photographic momento. David took a picture of me inside the archway, brown shoes neatly together, brown purse fondly cradled. We should not have been dressed like visiting academics, eager to gaze at poets' manuscripts behind doors in Italy. Robert Browning's love of the Italian landscape had sent him out into its streets and countryside where he found his *Dramatis Personae*. His characters spoke forcefully in the idiom of the time, leaping from the pages, like the young scamp in front of us, kicking his soccer ball against the walls of *Casa Guidi*.

I changed the fashionable footware for a pair of comfortable sneakers and headed down the dim back streets of Florence where Browning had found the furnishings for their apartment. In a warren of small workshops, craftsmen still forged iron chandeliers, chipped inlaid designs for marble tables, and decorated wooden chests. The open squares were lined with craftsmen's stalls offering high-quality gilded wooden trays and mirrors, hand-dyed marbelized writing papers and decoupaged boxes. Even though these vendors were basically operating souvenir stalls, their merchandise had been arranged with the same care given to museum exhibits. Smaller items were neatly piled in rectangular wicker baskets, arranged by colour or textural compatability, as structured as a verse in *tersa rima*. Browsers left with a respect for the merchandise even if they had not made a purchase.

In one of the crumbling corner buildings, a tortoiseshell cat sat on a pile of books in the dusty window of an English bookshop. As I approached to stroke her, the proprietor spoke from behind a pile of used books, "We call her Molly because she prefers to settle on that pile of

Joyce's work." Under the cat's curled body were James Joyce's epic tales of wandering and introspection. In the sort of odd illuminating flash that he favoured, I realized that he had strung together routine daily occurrences and small domestic scenes to forge a new sense of self in what have come to be recognized as the greatest works of twentieth century literature. There was a chance that Florence could have the effect of Dublin if we celebrated the poetry of the everyday.

Florentines are instinctive masters at yoking the mundane with the sublime. *Piazza della Signoria* with Michelangelo's marble *David* and Cellini's bronze *Perseus*, might pass for an outdoor gallery, if it weren't for the fact that football games, political riots and celebrations of municipal life regularly take place here. That scene in E.M. Forster's novel, *A Room with a View*, dramatizes this juxtaposition of the abstract with the concrete. A culturally inquisitive English heroine, Baedeker in hand, sets out for a day of sculpture-gazing, only to find herself involved in a brutal local squabble on this very public open space.

This connection between the world of art and the life of the street was even more evident inside the Uffizi Gallery. When I think of our visit there, I cannot separate the magnificent collection from the setting. Bottecelli's *Primavera* would be no less a work of genuis were it hanging in an airport, but viewing it suspended between a painted beamed ceiling and a marble floor, heightened its spirit. From the windows lining the long galleries, Florence under blue Italian skies, seemed more beautiful than the paintings. In one of these galleries, sun streams in on a mellow interior to spotlight white marble statues enthroned on elaborately carved plinths. At the end of this gallery, an elegant marble lady reclines, with all the time in the world to gaze on the Arno at her feet. It was a hauntingly beautiful interaction between static sculpture and living city.

Just beyond her, out of the window, I could see a corridor linking the art of the Uffizi to the commercial world along the top of the shop-lined *Ponte Vecchio* and the *Pitti Palace* across the river. That black silk dress splashed with vivid long-stemmed red tulips and brilliant yellow daffodils was still in the window of the boutique on the bridge. It was in my nature to feel guilty about admiring an object too much. Teachers are supposed to deal with concepts. But it seemed fitting that a corridor should link the Renaissance masters to the black silk dress on the *Ponte Vecchio*. They would have enjoyed painting a courtesan wearing it. Italian aesthetics were helping to melt the distinction between thoughts and things.

On our last day in Florence, we stood under an open arch on this historic bridge with a group of locals who were grabbing each other and gesticulating wildly towards a point far up the Arno River. I thought that they must be witnessing an apocalyptic disaster, but they were actually just exhibiting a typical Italian reaction to a parting in the clouds that was allowing a glimpse of the peaks of the Apennine range of mountains, glistening in the afternoon sun. "We're going through those brutes on the way to San Marino tomorrow," announced my sangfroid spouse.

March 25, 1969   SAN MARINO

Ever the optimist, I thought he meant a road skirting through a valley, or maybe one of those convenient tunnels that burrow from one side of a mountain range to the other. But the next day we did go through, or more accurately, over, those snow caps that had roused the watchers on the bridge. If there had been a tape deck in the van, Vivaldi's *Four Seasons* would have been the perfect score to accompany the trip that day. Heavy rain saw us out of Florence along the Arno. We climbed up into black clouds that lay in wisps on the road or got caught in smoky puffs in the bushes. Patches of snow appeared on the grass ahead. These grew into drifts several feet deep that covered the hillside. Tall, dark green firs, frosted at the tips, lent a Christmas spirit to the scene. I caught myself humming snatches of *Good King Wenceslas* as the fluffy white stuff started to obliterate the van. After half an hour of this winter wonderland, we came down to a small village where the sun blessed our picnic. Another ascent into the gods brought us to a barren peak. To heighten the feeling of solitude and cold isolation, we stopped, turned off the engine, and listened to the wind whistle around a steel grey stone monastery. The last lap carried us down burnt orange slopes of dried leaves, similar in mood to the autumnal furze on the Scottish highlands. On either side of this wooded river valley, towers rose on rocky heights.

I was on the watch for one town in particular, the Republic of San Marino, where we had decided to camp for the night. There was no mistaking this unique republic when it appeared. Houses, hotels, cars, telephone poles, all spiralling up a steep rock face, crowned by a partially rebuilt fort at the summit. This city state on the top of *Monte Titano*, has its own coinage and stamps. The glut of souvenir stalls had not yet strangled the town centre when we drove up to settle among the clouds for the night. First, a walk around the perimeter to take in the view that had made this a contentious lookout position during the Second World War. There lay the river valley, the Apennine range we had just crossed, and the Adriatic Sea, barely visible in the heavy mist that shrouded the entire panorama. Then, as though in benediction, an elusive sun slanted through the pink-tinged clouds resting uneasily on the jagged black peaks.

Back down at sea level the next morning, it was disconcerting to look up only to discover that our rocky campgrounds had been swallowed by clouds and mist. We must have been filling our lungs with rarefied air all night.

March 26, 1969   RAVENNA

We dipped our toes in the Adriatic at Rimini before heading up the coast to Ravenna. As we drove through an area choked by countless funnels belching sulphur fumes, petroleum factories and oil tanks, I bleated, "Don't tell me we're camping here tonight."

"No, the guide book says that there is a campsite near *Lido di Dante*. We're going through his hell right now. Brace yourself for the purgatory of the suburbs." These allusions to Dante's *Divine Comedy* reminded me that the primo Italian poet finished off this epic in Ravenna, before dying there in 1321. The camping grounds at *Marina di Ravenna* were *paradiso* - a fragrant pinewoods near the sea. David suggested that we go up towards the Basilica of San Francesco in search of Dante's tomb. This poet's intensity of emotion, his dreams of a united Europe and the enlightenment of its peoples, had brought many of our English poets to Italy centuries after his death. When we found the tomb near a secluded garden off a lovely square, we opened a bottle of *trebbiano di romagna*, wine from the region where he rested. Like Browning, he had been another man of the street, writing in the vernacular of his fellow citizens, fusing lofty visions with the minutiae of daily life. Stretched out in the tall grass, we drank to the message in his *Paradiso* - ultimate paradise comes from inner peace.

March 27, 1969   BOLOGNA

Bologna's reputation as the culinary capital of northern Italy merited a detour. Byron had summed it up in a nut shell as the home of "poets, painters and sausage." Locals label it *la rossa, la dotta, la grassa*, referring to its communist party leanings, its seat of learning and the fat in its diet. How could we resist a city that had given its name to Europe's oldest university (twelfth century) and the world's most popular deli meat, baloney. Actually, in Bologna, this king of deli meat is called mortadella, a sausage with the diameter of one of Saturn's moons. Although it has been made since the Middle Ages, the authentic Italian mortadella (pork sausage, fat and herbs pounded in a *mortar*) as approved by a Bolognese consortium, was not allowed into Canada until November of 2005. Italian-Canadian chefs were thrilled by its landing because now they could make authentic tortellini.

Far out on the highway we spotted one tall red brick tower, leaning ever so slightly eastward over red tiled roofs. As we closed in, we discovered its mate, fallen over, the remains tilted on a more decided angle. At one point the Bolognese, in a frenzy to keep up with the Joneses, had erected 180 of these towers, of which fifteen and a half remain. We were served the best cup of coffee of the trip under these leaning towers. If this was any indication, we'd better track down some of Bologna's more substantial specialities. Food emporiums were protected under medieval arcades, supported by intricately carved columns, erected to support the demand for student housing. Extra rooms had simply been added as extensions, jutting out of the front of buildings. Eighty per cent of the business district now offered this permanent umbrella to pedestrians. In one store window, rows of freshly made pasta lay like skeins of yarn on steel trays. Behind the counter, a woman was bent over a marble slab kneading egg, flour and water to make a ball of dough. Using an elongated, tapered wooden pin, she began to roll the lump into increasingly thin layers, until it was almost translucent. This was cut into tagliatelli and fettuccini noodles. An assistant lovingly shaped tortellini and wide slices for lasagna. We bought some raviolis stuffed with pumpkin and a container of their famous ragù, known to the rest of the world as sauce bolognese. This was one reputation that had lived up to its promise.

The original twin towers, medieval symbol of Bologna's powerful families.

MORTADELLA TORTELLINI

Recipes for this stuffed pasta go back to the fifteenth century. The city of Bologna has been making it with variations since that time. Generally, the stuffing includes minced chicken, ricotta, eggs, grated Parmesan and nutmeg, in addition to the mortadella. But I wanted to start out as simply as possible. You can always add to the mixture once you master the procedure.

INGREDIENTS

8 sheets of fresh pasta dough yields 32 three inch circles

1 eight ounce, 1/4 inch thick slice of mortadella

1 tablespoon ground pistachio nuts

a few gratings of fresh nutmeg

1/4 teaspoon coriander seeds ground

FOR SAUCE:

3 ounces melted butter

3 tablespoons thinly slivered fresh sage leaves

1 tablespoon lemon juice

1/2 cup freshly grated Asiago cheese

METHOD

1. Remove rind from mortadello. Cut into 1/2 inch chunks. Process in a machine with nuts and seasonings until very fine.

2. Most bought pasta sheets are too thick for ravioli and tortellini making. I compensate by running 10 inch by 5 inch sheets through the higher end of the steel rolling discs on our manual pasta maker until they become 14 inch by 5 inch. An easier alternative is to purchase

won ton wrappers, square or round. Their dough is thinner. Marco Polo brought the concept into Italy after his trip to China.

3. With a 3 inch crimped pastry cutter, form circles from the dough.

4. Brush the edges with cold water. Place a scant teaspoon of filling in the centre. Fold dough over to make a crescent shape. Press firmly all around to seal. Tuck the corners up to make the authentic tortellini shape if your dough is well enough sealed.

5. Place six at a time in a pot of boiling salted water. They will be cooked and floating on the surface within five minutes. Keep aside covered with a clean tea towel as the others cook.

6. Warm the sage and nutmeg in the melted butter with the lemon juice.

7. Gently lift pasta from boiling water in a fine strainer. Keep warm on a covered heated plate as you boil the remainder in batches.

8. Serve dressed with warm butter sauce and topped with grated Asiago or other hard Italian cheese of choice.

If you have left-over filling, stir in some mayonnaise and chopped dill pickle to make a baloney sandwich spread.

March 28, 1969   PADUA

The *Via Emilia*, the old Roman Road, cuts straight through Modena, where I discovered that vinegar can cost more than wine, and David discovered that Ferraris and Lamborghinis cost more than a house.

The British Automobile Association guide book calls the road to Padua, a flat monotonous road skirting the Euganean Hills. We broke the monotony with an excursion into these volcanic hills. After a climb up a narrow gorge through vineyards and woods, we were delighted to find ourselves in the small village of *Arquà Petrarch*, where there are two signs in the plaza. One directs you to the fourteenth century poet laureate's house, and the other to his tomb. In exile from Florence, Petrarch travelled across France, writing sonnets to Laura that would later influence Shakespeare and taking time out to climb Mont Ventoux. An early humanist, diplomat and scholar, he set the parameters for Renaissance man and earned his resting place here among the Euganean Hills. Near his pink marble sarcophagus, we lunched on a mortadella pannini and looked out on the same scene that had prompted Shelley to pen *Lines Written Among the Euganean Hills*.

Where we saw only a benign spring day with the warm Italian sun swelling the buds on this ancient hillside, Shelley saw a future of tyranny under Austrian rulers and ruin for the cities spread below on the plain of Lombardy. His prophesy for the two cities we were headed toward, Padua and Venice, were of special interest.

> *In thine halls the lamp of learning,*
> *Padua, now no more is burning.*

Mesopotamian scholars brought scientific knowledge, translations of the Greek and Roman classics and the Arabic numerical system to northern Italy at a time when Western Europeans needed to emerge from an earlier Dark Age. This infusion helped to make the University of Padua a beacon in a world searching for enlightenment. David set a challenge for our visit to Padua. "Let's see if Shelley's prophecy was accurate or if the lamps of learning are still burning in Europe's second oldest university."

In the *Piazza Prato della Valle*, an eliptical square, 78 statues of scholars, poets, scientists and philosophers border a narrow canal around a garden in the heart of Padua. Normally they set the tone for this city of learning. The day we arrived they had been upstaged by a huge striped circus tent sharing the square with them. We squeezed around an outdoor table with a group of circus clowns who recommended the local spritz, equal parts prosecco, soda and Campari. The crowd pouring out of the Big Top led us into a central quadrangle dominated by the highly decorative *Palazzo della Ragione*, originally a hall of justice and now the centre of a lively market area. Its surplus of balconies, columns, arches, and cherubims made it seem more like a Sultan's palace than a food market. On either side spread the fittingly named *Piazza della Frutta* and *Piazza della Erbe*, six rows of parchment and oyster-coloured canvas tenting under which carts sold vegetables, shoes and crockery. Shops under the pale ochre stone colonnades were crammed with meats, cheeses and the famed prosciutto, its curing process blessed by the sweet herbs on the hills. We bought some tortellini stuffed with spinach and a container of a creamy cheese sauce.

Under the shadows of the statues of scholars around the canal, as we set the pasta on to boil and heated the sauce on the camping stove, I asked David if the lamp of learning was still burning.

"Yes," replied my mate through a mouth full of pasta. "The streets are certainly bright with life."

Padua's legacy as a centre of learning also continues in the Univer-

Seventy-eight statues of ecclesiastics set the tone in this city of learning.

Produce spills out of the *Palazzo della Ragione* onto the the market square.

sity's school of medicine and its affiliation with the world's first botanical garden devoted specifically to medicinal plants. *The Orto Botanico de Padova*, established 1545, has been declared a World Heritage Site by UNESCO. Thousands of samples from all parts of the known world are laid out in geometric squares within an enclosed circular brick wall. Many plants originated in those same Euganean Hills where Shelley had sat musing. I wish I could let him know that they are not only thriving, but instructing medical students and botanists from around the globe. Homeopathic studies are alive and well.

March 29, 1969   VENICE

A quick map check that night confirmed we could reach Venice the next day. We opened the poetry book again to see what Shelley, back up on the Euganean Hills, had to say about this Queen of the sea:

> *Sun girt City, thou has been*
> *Ocean's child, and then his queen;*
> *Now is come a darker day,*
> *And thou soon must be his prey.*

Since those lines were written in 1818, we seem to have been doing all we can to hasten Venice into its watery grave. Here was the situation as I recorded it in my journal entry for March of 1969:

> *Two skylines are distinguishable as you come down the causeway connecting Venice to the mainland. One spews out black smoke from countless iron funnels and chimneys. Huge steel oil storage tanks, mazes of iron tubing and electrical circuits complete this horizon on the right. Ahead, over toward the left, lie the tenth century treasures of the Venetian Republic. A stately campanile, several golden Byzantine domes and a sea of red-tiled roofs compose this other landscape. The dirt, smoke and filth of this past century are threatening the existence of a medieval jewel in a precarious lagoon setting.*

Since our campsite was on the mainland near Mestre, we had plenty of opportunities to compare these contrasting scenes on daily runs into

Venice. Byron's lines that refer to a palace and a prison on either side of the Bridge of Sighs, could apply to these two larger landscapes. The finger of land connecting the palaces of *la Serenisima* to the prison of industrial waste was a crossing of sighs all the way. The sadness slips away once you board a vaporetto and slide around the first bend in the Grand Canal where twelfth century gilded marble palazzos float glimmering in the reflection of its water like a mirage. The magic continues as a black canopied gondola glides past with a coffin, followed by a barge full of wine bottles and telephone directories. Every commodity needed by the Venetians from their birth to their death must come over the water. The visitor can only gape at what they consider ordinary - a boat passing under the Academia bridge filled with white lilacs; children with schoolbags scurrying over the small stone bridges, as though it were perfectly natural to have water instead of cement on their streets. Our few days here were mostly spent riding up and down the canal - at twenty cents it was the best bargain in Europe.

Our other favourite activity was to claim a chair on *Piazza San Marco*, which John Ruskin correctly named, *the most beautiful room in Europe*. The first morning, we entered the square through a swagged archway at the end of one of the narrow *calli*. Everything was shrouded in mist. The *Campinale* was only half visible. Through the two columns that stand guard at the far edge, it seemed as though the world stopped, swallowed by sea and mist. Pale amethyst glass globes on tall light standards glowed with a mysterious delicacy. You have the sense of being in a grand ballroom, one wall formed by the exquisite golden façade of St.Mark's Basilica. Two competing restaurants supply musicians to keep the café society amused. We returned later that afternoon to take our place at one of *Quadri's* tables. A waiter brought two cappuccinos as *Florian's*, the competition on the other side of the square, started the concert. These string trios play with enough gusto to sound like mini orchestras in this space enclosed by architectural gems. *Some Enchanted Evening* bounced off the mosaic front of the basilica and sent thousands of pigeons swirling up among its five domes. The competing orchestras kept a continuous love song in the air.

The thousand year-old market under the arcades near the historic Rialto bridge, is serviced by canal barges that unload produce onto floating docks. In a quick half hour's shopping trip, we picked up *vitello de la mare* (a variation on tuna) at the amazing *pescheria* (fish stalls), ropes of garlic and red chillis, yellow tulips and mimosa, spinach-stuffed ravioli, and a hunk of parmesan. Vendors sang to each other as they arranged displays worthy of Tiffany's, while dealing with customers in a friendly banter. "That red lettuce and those broad beans are grown on the island of Erbosa, just out in the lagoon. You can't get fresher than picked this morning before sunrise." I loaded my basket with the ingredients for a light pot of minestrone - zucchini, red chard, green beans. The butcher shaved off beautiful slices of veal scaloppine then suggested we stop in at the tiny bar next door for a *cichetti e ombra* (snack and white wine). In this town, the snacks could be stuffed squid or a toasted crostini with *baccalà* (a creamy spread of salt cod and garlic). My epiphanic moment came as I reached out to stroke the sardines spiralled against each other in a circular wooden box at a fish stall facing the café. Ezra Pound's *The Study in Aesthetics* had materialized right there in front of me. In this poem, a young Italian street scamp, named Dante, hears his friends call out when a woman passes, *Ch'e be'a* (That's beautiful). He makes the same exclamation when he sees the sardines rowed up in their boxes. Beauty and harmony are recognizable in fish, as in women. Ezra Pound died a recluse in Venice, but a champion of modern aestheticism.

Café chairs fill the most beautiful outdoor room in Europe.

The archway at the base of the clock tower leads you into the maze of back canals. This photo was taken from the top of the Campanile.

MARKET MINESTRONE

Italians call a thin broth minestrina and a thick soup minestrone. The thickness can come from pasta, rice, bread, beans or a mixture of these. I prefer to thicken by puréeing the beans. A variety of herbs and vegetables, gathered from the market in season, float in the thick soup.

INGREDIENTS
2 tablespoons olive oil
1 leek finely minced (3/4 cup)
1 red onion finely minced (3/4 cup)
1 carrot cut into small dice (3/4 cup)
1 cup of potatoes cut into 1/4 inch cubes
1/2 cup of diced celery
2 cups Savoy cabbage (the one with dark green curly leaves) shredded fine
1/2 cup chopped fennel root (optional)
1 tablespoon fresh oregano leaves
1/4 cup flat Italian parsley, chopped
6 cups of broth or water - Italian cooks prefer a beef stock for the depth of flavour it gives the soup. A piece of smoked ham would work as would a good chicken stock. If opting for water, consider adding a vegetable/herbal stock cube. We kept a supply in the van.
2 - 14 ounce tins of drained, organic Navy beans or soak and boil 1-1/2 cups dried white beans the day before preparing the soup
1 bulb (about 6 to 8 cloves) of garlic roasted in olive oil
6 fresh sage leaves finely sliced
2 teaspoons coarse salt
6 grinds black pepper

ROASTED GARLIC
1. Preheat oven to 325F.
2. Place garlic bulb in a small ovenproof dish or casserole.
3. Pour 2 tablespoons of olive oil over it.
4. Cover and bake 30 minutes or until the cloves feel soft when pierced with a knife.
5. Remove skins from cloves. Keep them in the oil until needed.

DICED TOMATOES
You can prepare this in the oven at the same time as you roast the garlic. Or open a tin of diced Roma tomatoes.
1. Wipe the dust from freshly picked garden plum tomatoes.
2. Pack 8 of them tightly into a lidded casserole. No need to take the skins off. The heat will do that.
3. Bake one-half hour for a small amount or one hour for a large pot full that you can freeze in batches for future use.
4. Let cool until you can slip the skins off and cut into pieces - 2 cups will be enough for this soup.

METHOD
1. Warm the olive oil in the bottom of a large stock pot.
2. Add the vegetables and herbs in the order given, allowing several minutes, stirring to coat each one in the oil.
3. Pour on the broth and bring to a simmer for 30 minutes.
4. Stir in the cooked navy beans.
5. Add the roasted garlic cloves, the 2 cups diced tomatoes, salt, pepper and sage.
6. Simmer for 30 minutes.
7. Transfer half of the soup to another large pot or bowl. Purée with an immersion blender or pass through the largest disc of a food mill.
8. Stir back into the soup.
9. While heating together gently, toast slices of crusty Italian bread

brushed with olive oil.

10. Grate some fresh Parmesan to sprinkle on each bowl.

Even the mundane coffee and doughnut is transformed into an experience in Italy. In our bar of choice, we would squeeze in beside business men, chatting in their white shirts and suits, gulping down the required caffeine fix, to place our order for *machiatti* and warm jam-filled brioche which was baked in a small kitchen behind the front of the store. The scent of freshly gound coffee beans and yeasty sweet rolls baking, is reason enough to cross the Atlantic. Our rich, dark espresso with a jet of steamed milk, was served in delicate blue and white flowered demi-tasses. Styrofoam just no longer cuts it.

Our last night, we were late getting back to the mainland and opted for a restaurant meal at a small place near Mestre. The waitress was very pleased to have out-of-towners as she wanted to try a new dish on us. As I sat waiting for a plate of risotto in squid ink, or perhaps a variation on pasta vongole, she appeared with a large pizza. " This is a southern Italian specialty. We're introducing it up here. Do you think it will catch on?" At least it was a novel rendition, with artichokes and anchovies, which have become two of our standard ingredients on homemade pizzas.

Another surprise waited outside the van when we woke up the next morning. David peered through a slit in the curtains to exclaim, "The armies of the night have descended." We were surrounded by thirty tents of Portugese students. He negotiated the van carefully through the bivouac wondering whether or not their stay would be free too. No one had ever shown up at this site to collect fees. Another officially closed Italian campsite.

GREEK STYLE PIZZA

We were edging as close to the east as we would get on this trip. Different ingredients were suggesting themselves. Amounts of the following will vary according to personal taste and size of the pizza.

INGREDIENTS
a rectangle of flatbread made with olive oil - these are available pre-made
2 small Japanese eggplants
oil for dribbling and basting
feta cheese
black kalamata olives
preserved artichoke hearts
anchovies
circles of thin kielbasa if you wish
crumbled dried oregano

METHOD
1. Preheat oven to 400F.
2. Lightly baste base with olive oil.
3. Prepare the ingredients by cutting the cheese into small squares, pitting and halving the olives.
   Cut the artichokes and anchovies in half.
4. Cut the eggplant into thin slices. Baste with oil. Grill a few minutes per side.
5. Arrange ingredients on the dough. Sprinkle with oregano. Dribble with oil.
6. Bake until base is crisp and cheese is melted - 10 to 15 minutes.

April 1, 1969   TRIESTE

We did not dip down to tickle the toes in Italy's boot, prefering to hug the coastal route that ran towards Yugoslavia. This last stretch of Italian coastline was more attractive than the earlier stretch we had travelled. Dark green pine trees bordered cliffs that plunged toward the teal blue Adriatic. There was even a well-equipped campsite a few miles before Trieste, at the small village of Sistiana. Caravans fringed the rocky shore, sheets flapping in the breeze, which meant that hot water would be available. We soon had our laundry line strung up with the rest of them and the van soaped down for its upcoming northern adventures.

I woke up feeling very relaxed, content and warm. Sun beat in through the yellow-checked curtains and the sea lapped at our side. The entire area was embraced by two huge arms of rock. David explored the honeycombed tunnels and gun emplacements of this once strategic point and returned with some surprising news. "At the camp store I picked up a map of a walking trail along the cliffs that leads to the site of Duino Castle where the poet Rilke wrote while visiting the owner." I knew nothing of Rilke or his writings. Since our *Oxford Book of Verse* was no help with a German poet, we went into town in search of a bookstore.

Trieste stands at the crossroads of two empires on the border with Slovenia - not fully Italian, still clinging to memories of its importance as an Austro-Hungarian port. We spent hours ambling streets lined with elegant Austrian Belle Époque buildings. An Art Nouveau warehouse on the wharf holds an aquarium and a fish market. The owner of a small bookstall explained to us that this most cosmopolitan of Italian cities, where European cultures mixed, was the perfect milieu for Rilke. We carried a book of his poems to a café on the canal. He clinched our Italian experiences in his "object poems," crystal clear descriptions of things, which could only be appreciated he maintained, once you had run the gamut of experience, from small wildflowers to large cities. Perfect. We could make a living dealing with small things we found while travelling between large cities and smelling the roses. This may not have been the interpretation he had in mind, but it kept us happy for the next thirty-three years. In his poem, *Archaic Torso of Apollo*, he wrote, You must change your life. Could any instruction be clearer?

Perhaps Trieste appealed to us because we felt out of time, out of place. We sat for a few sunny hours by the sea, eating pastries and drinking Valpolicella. Or maybe it was because this city had attracted modern exiles, the most renowned being James Joyce. In a series of rented flats here in the first decade of the twentieth century he wrote *Portrait of the Artist as a Young Man*, a definitive comment on the interior journey in search of the self. My journal records that we felt at home here.

Flash Forward

Italy had cast its spell, and after we had opened our business, we returned for stays of at least one month in an old casa, to areas not covered on this initial two-week camping tour. Two of these visits to Tuscany, are worth including here to present a more rounded picture of this rich country.

CHIANTI
February/March, 1975

Our first store in London, Ontario was near an art school, where we made friends with a few for whom life was a banquet on a tight budget. Between sips of red wine at an artist's opening party, Alice casually mentioned, "Steve and I have rented a farmhouse in Chianti for a year. Why don't you and David come over?"

"Don't ever say that to us unless you mean it, because we'll take you up on it"

"I'm serious. See you at *Casa Martino*."

The letter that Alice sent a few months later intrigued us even more.

"The house is not what I thought it would be. The tower in the photo is really a pigeon coop. One of the floors is a stable. I live in the kitchen (as large as your store) to keep warm near the fireplace (as large as your van). There are many empty bedrooms. Come anytime. It's a shame not to fill them."

The thought of jetting into a set from Amarcord acted as an incentive rather than a deterrent.

Practicalities like, *Will we find the house without a number or a street? Will anyone be there? Will we be disappointed.....?* were replaced by an Italian sit-com on the train between Roma and Firenze. I had asked the refreshment vendor for a glass of wine to ease my paranoia. *Non possible.* Two virile, dark-haired Sicilians sitting across from us darted a beam of pure mischief and asked the vendor for an orangeade. As soon as the cart had rolled past, they leapt onto the seat, pulled down a carton, pressed open a switch blade and extracted a bottle of *vino rosso*. "Our own grapes", they boasted, as they mixed a version of sangria. Out came a mouth organ and the party was rolling.

It was dusk by the time we crossed the piazza in Florence from the train station to the bus stop where we boarded the suburban line marked *Greve*. The driver serenaded us with Verdi arias as he dropped regular commuters off in the middle of inky black country roads. Eventually we were his only audience as he worked his way through *La Fortunato del Destino*, carrying us deeper into the hills. At last he made a terminal stop in the centre of a triangular town square that we recognized from post-cards as Greve. Two young scamps were trying to tie firecrackers onto a dog's tail. In a bar under a stone arch we asked for directions to *Casa Martino*.

A si, signore. You'll need a car.

Soon we were installed in a large Fiat limo that served as the local taxi. It began an unsettling ascent, weaving through medieval castle towns, scattering loose pebbles into the gorges that dropped away inches from the Fiat's wheels. Tightly closed shutters barred any chink of welcome in the few remote farmhouses. The black night contained twenty billion stars and two Canadians whirling with their Samsonite luggage through a vacuum. The driver pounded on a few bolted doors. *Non Canadese*. Finally, a beam of light from a hilltop house guided us to Alice, sitting inside a ten-foot wide fireplace with a plate of freshly steamed spinach, chickpeas and osso bucco. Steve immediately offered a glass of the current year's Chianti, young, honest and pure, which eased any remaining apprehensions like skin from a snake.

CHICKPEAS WITH
SPINACH AND SHANKS

Alice had been reheating left-overs from a veal shank when we surprised her with our arrival. A few extra handfuls of chickpeas and spinach leaves extended the bits of meat for company. This hearty meal can be based on lamb or beef cuts with the bone in. One of our local butchers is married to an Ecuadorian. They make good use of all cuts of meat. The package that contained this beef was labelled "Soup Bones" but had enough meat on the bone for four servings and the delicious marrow was a bonus.

INGREDIENTS

2/3 cup dried chickpeas
2 cloves crushed garlic
1 tablespoon olive oil
1 small white onion, chopped
2 cuts of beef, lamb or veal 1" thick left on the shank bone
1 cup beef broth
4 plum tomatoes
2 cups washed spinach
salt and pepper

METHOD

1. Rinse the chickpeas. Sort out any small stones or irregular beans. Cover with water to soak.
2. After an hour or so, drain and cover with fresh water to soak four hours or overnight.
3. Drain. Use fresh water and bring to a boil in the saucepan with some

salt and the crushed garlic.

4. Depending on the length of your pre-soak, they can be tender in half an hour. Otherwise, keep on a simmer until they are fairly soft. Set aside.

5. In a large skillet which has a lid, soften the chopped onion in oil. Dry the meat, push onions aside and brown the meat.

6. Pour the broth into the skillet. Use a wooden spatula to incorporate any bits into the broth. Cover and simmer for two hours until meat is tender.

7. Remove meat to a saucepan while you boil down the liquid in the skillet to thicken slightly. Add seasonings if the broth did not have salt.

8. Pour broth over meat in the waiting pan. (Alice kept it warm beside the fire.)

9. Combine the drained chickpeas, chopped tomatoes and spinach leaves in the skillet. Season.

10. Place beef on a plate with vegetable mixture at the side. Drizzle with broth.

As the *gallo nero* crowed, Alice tossed a handful of pebbles against the shutters to let us know it was market day. She handed us a sweet roll and a basket to carry down through the vineyards to the triangular square. Life had flooded in overnight. In full glorious technicolour, wagons of produce crammed the space. A heady mix of aromas assaulted our deprived senses: the tang from a pile of citrus; the sour, briny odour of olives; dark-roasted, freshly ground espresso beans; a rush of warm rosemary focaccia from the *forno*. Over it all, savory whiffs of roasted pork drew us hypnotically to the pig van. The entire animal lay staring at us, its crackled skin pierced and stuffed with garlic, rosemary, sage and fennel. If he could speak, he'd say *Eat me*. Ask for a *panetini piquante* and you are handed a freshly baked crusted roll, sliced and expertly filled by a master carver with lean slices of pork, bits of the liver and kidney, some crispy fat, garlic and coarse salt. Take it into the café, lean casually against the bar, and savour it with a glass of Chianti. Your attitude towards grocery shopping will be changed forever.

Into the basket we tossed picnic fare - a small pecorino from the sheep we had passed on the way downhill, fennel sausages, bread from Mario's forno, a litre of 1973 Uzzano. Near *Castello San Martino*, we sank down into a hillside of sweet dried hay and let the Italian sun seep into our souls.

Back at our six hundred year-old farmhouse, whose age really did compensate for the absence of heat or water pressure, we would empty the rest of the market baskets onto the table. "Let's roast the quail stuffed with sage over the fire tonight."

Nothing ever daunted Alice in this kitchen with no stove. She was our Susanna Moodie on locale. After a visit to Siena, she even dared try her hand at making a *panforte*, the national dolce with pounds of glazed fruits and nuts.

Sleeping arrangements were creative. Instead of thread count, Alice made a hasty sheet count. "Now let's see. We have three sheets and four bedrooms. Steve's sister arrives tomorrow. The back bedroom has bits and pieces of an Etruscan well scattered over the floor. Do you think you two can sort something out?"

"We'll manage. Coats make fine blankets."

The next morning we were awakened by a farm worker rattling his tools out of the cave under our bedroom. Steve was washing out a large straw-covered demi-john on the terrace.

"Give me a hand would you? We're going to take this up to *Montefioralle* and have the castello fill it." Alice was tearing newspaper into strips. "Roll those up tightly Ann. They will be our corks when we re-bottle the bulk wine. I'll start washing out the bottles."

The only glitch to the success of this proposed expedition was the old Cinquecento toward which David and Steve were hefting the fiask. It would only start while coasting downhill. "Give us a push from the top of the hill. Run along beside it and hop in." Steve explained as he slid behind the wheel. And so I found myself hugging a rotund green bottle in the back seat as we careened around the corkscrews that led to the medieval stone village of *Montefioralle*.

It took two of us to lift the knocker on the large carved wooden door. "Is it possible to have our fiask filled?" "*Si.*"

Inside we were surrounded by large wooden casks holding 1974 Chianti. The flask was weighed on a giant iron scale, filled by a hose attached to a clear plastic drum, then weighed again. Seven thousand lire, about nine dollars for twenty-seven bottles. Such a bargain we felt obliged to buy a few 1971 *reservas*. The Cinquecento rolled back to the house where I held the funnel, Alice passed the bottles and Steve and David poured. A dribble of special oil seals the top before the cork is inserted. White angel hair removes any trace of this oil before the wine is poured. Our cellar was stocked for the duration.

Outings into the Tuscan countryside cinematically spanned a broad emotional gamut - from an evening mass among frescoes, with bells, incantations and monks bearing thick ivory candles, to stag night at the Greve cinema showing *The Highschool Girl*, removing her clothing as the opening credits rolled.

These expeditions took on an added frisson when the Cinque lost its gears completely in Siena. David pushed it down a muddy hill in a light Sienese drizzle. Three of us pushed it back up for three more tries - no go. A truck driver had to jump start us because we were blocking the highway. Once rolling, we sang, recited Italian poetry and consumed an entire roast chicken in the back seat. Absolutely nothing could dampen our spirits - until the day the car completely died, packed with our fire wood. Rare leg of lamb held no appeal. By divine intervention two archangels, disguised as young Italians, transferred our load, drove us home, and took Steve to rip the gear box out of a wrecked car while we started the fire to roast the lamb.

UNCOOKED PASTA SAUCE

There is a villa on the next hill that opens its kitchen to guests. Mama brought a fragrant bowl to our table with warm fettucini noodles that she had rolled and cut that day. But she was lyrical about her sauce - "not cooked, all fresh." She proceeded to describe how to prepare it.

INGREDIENTS
To serve four:
1/3 cup olive oil
2 cloves garlic
4 large, fresh basil leaves
2 large garden tomatoes or 4 tinned Italian plum tomatoes if it is not the season
1 tablespoon balsamic vinegar
1 teaspoon salt
several grinds black pepper
1/8 teaspoon dried chilli flakes
6 black Kalamata olives, pitted
1/3 cup mozzarella cheese cut into small cubes
a chunk of Parmesan cheese which you can grate (a huge taste difference over the packaged)
2 ounces fresh fettucini noodles per person

METHOD
1. Pour the oil into a large pasta serving bowl which has been warmed in hot water or a low oven.
2. Slice the garlic into the oil in thin pieces.

3. Add the tomatoes chopped.
4. Cut or chop the basil leaves. Add to the bowl.
5. Stir in the vinegar.
6. Slice the olives. Add to the other ingredients with the seasonings.
7. Let everything macerate while the water boils for the pasta.
8. Fresh pasta requires only a few minutes to cook in a large pot of rapidly boiling water.
9. Test a strand to see if it is to your taste. Drain and add immediately to the bowl of sauce.
10. Stir the cubed mozzarella into the hot noodles so that it will melt.
11. Serve in warmed bowls. Grate fresh Parmesan on top.

We returned that same September for the wine harvest. One night as we were crouched around the hearth gnawing on roast rabbit, Steve yelled from the back room, "*Montefioralle* is ablaze on its hill." We chugged up the road and landed in the midst of *Ballo Popolare al Castello*. Stone walls, intended to hold back invaders, now held antique iron saucer-lamps whose wicks flared from crude oil. In the piazza, *una tipica orchestrina accompagnera le danze* and the only wallflower was nona tapping time with her cane on the iron bench. In a frenzied whirl, tangos, charlestons, fox trots and street dances followed one another under the wavering torch flares from the towering walls. Casks with spigots fuelled the revels with a continous flow from this vintage year.

TUSCANY
March, 2007

A 2003 Chianti Colli Senesi, a DOCG wine made from the grapes growing on our rented property on the hills below *Montefollonico*, was waiting for us on the walnut table when we opened the tall glass doors into the kitchen. It bore a descriptive label:

> *Dalla vigna del Mulinello sulle colline assolate che guardano Montepulciano dalla parte de Tempio di San Bagio Prodotto e Imbattigliato da Agienda Agricola le Capanne di Sopra, Montefollonico*

This explains that the grapes were grown on this agrifarm on the side of the hill near the domed Renaissance temple of San Bagio, part of the panoramic views of the valley and hilltown of *Montepulciano* visible from our windows. Every morning I would open the wooden bedroom shutters a crack to allow a blinding ray of light to wake us from the type of deep sleep possible only when surrounded by absolute silence. Opening them wider, it seemed that *Montepulciano* had vanished during the night. The valley had filled like a cauldron with bubbling white mist, puffs of it brushing the sides of our casa. The rows of cypress, the olive and wine groves, are as drenched in this foam as they were millions of years ago when this *Val di Chiano* was under water.

Our landlord could not have given us a more welcome gift than one of his own wines. We needed it that first night. This property, perched on its own promontory at the end of a very steep gravel road (sign warns drivers DEAD SLOW), took some time to find. All of the stores in the village at the top of the hill were closed for Sunday, except The Bar Sport, where all eyes were rivetted to the televised running of the *Tour d'Italia*. One young chap who spoke a few words of English, grasped our desperation and told us to follow him to the housekeeper. She opened the iron doors that cover the three sets of long French windows leading from the terraced garden. Inside was well appointed with antique family pieces, but cold, as one would expect a stone house to be in March. Will I never learn? I immediately sensed that with the tile floors, high brick and beam ceilings and three bedrooms, I did not make an economical choice, yet again. Heating could be ruinous. None of these grim practicalities had swayed my decision once I saw the photo of the kitchen fireplace in their listing, with the bonus of a large stone log-burning hearth in the sitting room. But we had no paper or wood, no matches, no food and it was still Sunday. Thus the significance of that bottle of wine left on the kitchen table.

Standing next to this now empty bottle under the kitchen window, is a litre of organic *olio extra virgine* from the neighbouring farm owned by Robert Vaughan. We had walked down his gravel path to get some foraging suggestions that first day, and were thrilled to find that:

(i)   He was English so we could dispense with charades.
(ii) He not only produced this splendid oil, but also wine and vinsanto.
(iii) He gave us a box of fire starters.
(iv) He told us we could open the door of the bank with our credit card, thus gaining access to the bank machines.
(v)   Once we had money we could buy milk, bread and water at The Bar Sport.
(vi) He told us to raid the yellow municipal recycling bins for newspaper and cartons to start our fires.

A mine of information was our Robert. In a province famed for its

Our rented farmhouse set in the hills below *Montefollonico*.

The Val di Chiano, drenched in morning mist,
as seen from the bedroom window.

wine and its oil, this first find was in no way disappointing. We did not need to go far to find ambrosial olive oil. Bob Vaughan eighteen years ago became part of this landscape, planting, nurturing, harvesting and producing excellent quality organic oil, wine, and vin santo, in small batches. We left his farm with a litre of each. The oil tasted of fresh grass, so green, so fruity, like sampling a mouthful of landscape.

His unlabelled wine bottle stands next to his excellent olive oil bottle. He sold us his vino, pressed through a traditional wooden device, for a few euros, explaining that he considers it "bread" wine as opposed to "book" wine, a distinction that sorts out wine types better than many others I have come across. He prefers to quaff it with a hearty local loaf. To my taste, it was full-bodied enough to go down well with a book. There is still some of his pale yellow *vin santo* left in the next bottle. The half-litre one beside it holds a dribble of Bob's grappa.

The empty bottle labelled, *2004 Montefioralle, Chianti Classico*, bears testimony to the fact that our first day on the road we made it up to this hill town en route to the farmhouse beyond Siena. This town near Grève, in which we had spent that halcyon month so many years ago with friends, had become prettier, less elemental, more like a set from *Romeo and Julliete*, balconies teeming with geraniums around every corner. Not something to complain about really.

The remaining empties on the counter come from the surrounding *Montes*, all renowned for not only their wines, but a range of high quality local products. In the pages of a beautiful, marbelled journal, purchased in Florence to hold a daily record of our time in Italy, I decide that since we are staying in an ideal location, I will inventory the best Tuscany has to offer. Each day we travelled no further than twenty miles to find a town, a wine, a garden, a product, a store, that qualified as the best in this province. The hill we are sitting on, is one of a circle of six hills, each crowned with a village or a town, separated by only a dozen or so kilometres. There was enough time for a morning market visit, an alfresco lunch and an afternoon's exploration, before returning home, where the find of the day could be prepared over a wood fire in our traditional kitchen.

That room was the main reason I booked this house with its three bedrooms and two bathrooms. Definitely too large for just two people, but how else was I to get a kitchen with chestnut beams, red terra-cotta tile floors, a fireplace at waist height and french doors leading onto a terrace of herbs, almonds and olives? On one of the white walls, a tall walnut armoire holds all the glassware, dishes, pots, pans and equipment we need. No cookware for foreign cuisine intrudes among the pasta pots and cheese platters. Under a casement window, which frames a view of the valley, a pair of stainless steel sinks are set in the long white marble counter top, so that I enjoy a vista while chopping, slicing or washing-up. The spirit of the land infuses an Italian kitchen. Produce grown a few feet outside the doors dominates the cuisine - oil, grapes, rosemary, parsley, lemons, almonds, truffles, wild boar - unbelievably all sharing

Robert Vaughan, who owned the neighbouring farm, filled bottles of his *organic olio extra virgine*, his *vinsanto* and his *bread* wine for us.

this promontory of land with us.

The other noted specialty of the area is pecorino cheese, made from the milk of ewes grazing on our hillside. At the small restaurant up in our village, they presented us with a plate of sliced pecorino, pears, and *millefiori* honey, made from the thousand flowers and herbs of the terrain. They were so sure that customers would like this dessert, that they stocked wheels of the cheese and jars of the honey by the door. We bought both.

The lady butcher near the old wall at the entrance to the village, chuckled when I chose four tiny lamb chops to grill on our fire. She called them *bambini*. While David chopped the wood, I gathered an intensely fragrant bouquet of sage, thyme, bay and rosemary from our garden. A local man walked by me with his dog sniffing the earth. "Are you hoping to find truffles?" I asked. He brought a handful from his pocket, worth a king's ransom. "This area is noted for them," he explained. The next day, we had them shaved thinly on top of homemade pasta in a small restaurant. The term "Eat Local" must have originated here, and nowhere could you do it better.

It took an effort of will to drag ourselves off our hill to start visiting the necklace of other hilltowns that surrounded us. *Montepulciano*, the medieval town that straggles up a volcanic ridge facing us across the valley, is noted for its *vino nobile*, a wine for lords, but I was in search of Signor Mazzetti's *Bottega del Rame*, the finest maker of copper pots, utensils, and decorative accessories in the region. Climb up and up the main cobblestoned strada until you spot a very large, round copper shield emblazoned with grapes, hanging in front of a long, narrow store.

Inside, every inch is covered with sauteuses for ragus, frypans for escalopes, saucepans for minestrone, all catering quality, all hand forged and tin lined by Sr. Mazzetti, who proudly explained that he is the fourth generation devoted to this craft. He offered to take us to his workshop and volunteered a discount on items to be shipped. Here was a man who was accustomed to buyers setting up idealized top-quality stores.

The kitchen fireplace was my main reason for choosing this house.

Behind the bar at *Latte di Luna*.

Another day, another hill town, several more bottles for the collection growing under our window. *Montalcino* dispenses samples of the renowned *Brunello* wine from a massive fortress that straddles a high strip of rock. From the dizzy heights of this National Wine Library, you can sip a heady, rich *Brunello*, while gazing down on the terraces that provided the grapes.We asked the pourer in the *Enoteca* for directions to *Caffè Fiaschetteria Italiana*, the 1888 landmark created by Ferruccio Biondi Santi which retains the red velvet sofas, nouveau-style mirrors and yellow marble tables of the period. Plates of chicken liver crostini, bowls of funghi and bean soup, were perfect accompaniments for the strong wines.

Every town was distinctive - the hair-raising climb to the summit of *Cortona; Bagno Vignoni*, where popes bathed their feet in the rectangular spa-pool that forms the city-centre; and *Chianciano Terme*, setting for Fellini's movie, 8 & 1/2; until finally we found a perfect Renaissance town. If you are on a quest for the ideal, you will find it in *Pienza*, a humanist utopia, modelled on an urban plan by Pope Piccolomini and his architect in 1485. Harmony rules - from the gracious palazzos, spacious piazzas, to the flower-decked five-hundred year old houses on streets with fairytale names: *Via dell'Amore* - Street of Love; *Via del Bacio* - Street of a Kiss; *Via della Fortuna* - Street of Fortune. From the tranquil loggia of the Pope's secret garden you look out over his structured topiary, across the *Val d'Orcia* to Mount Amiata.

It is fitting that the definitive trattoria would be situated at the end of *Via San Carlo* in this tiny perfect town. Only two seats were left for lunch at the bustling *Latte di Luna*, whose short menu features wild boar in pasta, ragus and stews. David felt he was getting revenge on the wild boar whose snorting had suprised him several nights earlier while he was star-gazing on the terrace. There are many of these animals roaming the forests and farmlands of this area, so hunters consider them fair game and they turn up in sausages and sauces. After three slices of the house gelato, we made our way toward the bar near the exit where there were photographs of Juliette Binoche, Ralph Fiennes and Anthony Minghella. The Italian scenes in *The English Patient*, were shot in a neighbouring villa. The stars had supped on The Milk of the Moon.

A dried poppy sits in the last bottle in the row. We plucked it from the verge along the edge of one of the region's many *strada bianco*, small white country road/laneways that criss-cross the fields around us. This particular one connects our house with *La Foce*, the famous garden and estate of the Origo family. The name means meeting place, due to the conflux of several roads. On a personal level, this enchanted garden, set down in a stark patch of the *Val d'Orcia*, connected stray threads from my life. More lunar than Tuscan, the landscape reminds me of Scotland's barren moorlands. These alien, rounded hillocks have been given the name *crete senesi*. Near the end of the Second World War, my father's Scottish regiment had battled their way up through this area to help liberate Tuscany.

I sat on the grass of our darkened terrace that night, staring across the valley at *Montepulciano* under a full peach moon, surrounded by stars in a midnight blue sky. In spite of the turbulence of history, the natural rhythms of this timeless landscape wrap me in a sense of eternal peace.

AUSTRIA
Snow and Music

April 2, 1969 THE DOLOMITE MOUNTAINS

The arrival of April signalled that it was safe to leave the edges of the sea and move north (we thought). I had forgotten T.S. Eliot's dire forecast that it could be the cruellest month, although he may not have been referring to the nasty weather. We had expected the Latin spring to continue to blossom. Instead, Celtic blasts nipped it in the bud. We drove up into the Dolomites and the Austrian Alps, following a valley road which bordered a pristine mountain stream, pale, pale aqua with a hint of iciness in its froth as it twisted like a chiffon scarf through spongy green pockets of grass and moss at the base of the mountains. As we rose higher, the rain which had plagued us from Trieste, froze and became a full fledged snow storm. Our world became Tyrolean: timber A-frames with stencilled balconies; felt hats on every head; leather pants on men and boys; oxen pulling large farm carts; Strauss' portrait on the one hundred schilling notes. The Citroens and Fiats had been replaced by Mercedes-Benzes and Volkswagens. The van radio optimistically pumped out Viennese waltzes in spring time.

Our first Austrian campsite was in a farmyard built against the fortifications of an old walled city. We had a view of the onion-domed church towers in the centre of town and the shell of an old monastery looming from the hill above it. When we awoke the next morning, this entire tableau was covered in several inches of snow, difficult to clean off the windows while still in pyjamas. The van had been transformed into an igloo, not unlike a room in one of the new breed of "ice hotels".

Thankfully, the Shell station nearby had hot water. We were so grateful, we signed up for a Shell credit card.

Vienna was only 150 miles away, but it was over two mountain passes. The first one was a series of relatively insignificant grades, but the Schillering Pass had one switchback too many. David pulled out to pass a twenty-foot transport as an eighteen wheeler came bearing down in the left-hand lane.

"David, if you want to keep breathing, you'd better step on it."

"The pedal's on the floor. She hasn't got any more to give."

Our van was rattling at its maximum speed when the truck driver correctly assessed the gravity of the situation and applied his brakes just enough to allow us to squeeze between them with centimeters to spare. I looked out the back window expecting to see our mangled van on the road, confirming the eerie sensation that I had just become one of Noel Coward's blithe spirits. This near-miss made us aware of the frailty of life. It almost felt as though our mental decision to start a new life had been given the physical blessing of a fresh start.

Our route through the Dolomite Mountains from Italy to Austria.

April 3, 1969 VIENNA

At the end of that day, fate brought us to the most calming camp ground of the trip, exactly when we needed it most. The Viennese washrooms were warmer than Cuba and my body savoured a hot shower as though it were a baptism. A long communal cooking-eating room was part of the facility. Over a restorative cup of tea within a circle of warm stoves, we caught up on road news with fellow campers from Germany, Denmark and the Netherlands. We agreed that France was about Food, Italy had Art and they assured us that Austria was Music. In this capital city the Merry Widow waltzed continually and the Danube was always blue. They told us which tram car to catch for the ride into the centre of Vienna and we hopped on board, raring to kick up our heels in three-four time.

The broad sweeping avenues of this former capital of the Hapsburg Empire were wide enough to be dance floors, but the monumental buildings surrounded by acres of park and the general tone of imperialistic grandeur were not conducive to street dancing. The Emperor Franz Joseph embarked on an ambitious building project that lasted over twenty years and replaced medieval walls with a spectacular circle of dramatically grand buildings. The opera house, the parliament buildings, city hall, theatres, museums, a university, the stock exchange, the banks, and all of the *grand palais* of the elite who ruled these offices, was called the *Ringstasse*.

The city presented a very conservative public face. Felt hats with little feathers stuck in the brim nodded on every head. Loden green mountain capes or coats with full pleated backs covered tweed skirts or wool trousers. Feet were firmly laced into brown brogues. The tram let us off at the *Messe Platz*, a large garden of rigorously pruned conical hedges. When we stepped onto the manicured lawn, a conscientious burgher chastised us. A massive statue of the Empress Maria -Theresa beamed down in approval of this stricture. The impressive buildings of the Imperial Natural History Museum and the Imperial Art Museum were interspersed by equally formidable parks and statuary.

But this was also the romantic capital of carriage rides in a fiacre, stone fountains in front of gilt palaces; ball gowns swirling under glittering chandeliers to Strauss or the sentimental Franz Lehar. A whiff of this city of dreams can be found in the famous coffee houses that have assumed a literary, political and musical presence since the introduction of coffee by Turkish invaders in the seventeenth century. Local bakers even fashioned their rolls in the crescent shape of the Ottoman empire, giving the world croissants. These cozy meeting places have provided an intimate refuge from the monumental and grandiose, where townsfolk can pursue their specific passions, undisturbed in congenial surroundings. Students and intellectuals meet at Café Hawelka whose walls are papered with current posters, including, on the day we visited it, one which read, *a chance to dance*. So this was still the city of fancy footwork. Newspapers and magazines hung from wooden poles on the wall. *Hausfrauen* in fur hats had reconnoitered the tables at *Café Pruckl* for an afternoon of bridge. At other spots we tried, tables were given over to chess or board games or billiards. No one disturbs you all day.

These are not the hole-in-the-wall snugs which you might find down an Italian back street. They are significant buildings anchoring a corner or commanding a dominant place on a main block. Their decor reflects the tastes of their clientele. The *Café Sperl*'s fourteen foot windows, swagged with brocaded draperies, are set into panelled walls. We took a seat at one of the round marble tables to read a brochure on the former famous patrons. Johann Strauss played in this café where Wagner, Chopin and Liszt may well have dropped in to hear the latest music.

In the 1890s a group of revolutionary architects and progressive artists who seceded from the establishment, met in this café to discuss plans for a dramatic new building in which they could exhibit the avant Secessionist style of art. We located it over beside the Academy of Fine Arts. This group obviously preferred geometric design, the rectangles and squares of Charles Rennie Mackintosh, as opposed to the floral swirls of Horta or Guimard. Josef Olbrich, one of the movement's founders, had challenged the standard baroque and rococo of the rest of the city, by introducing this orientalized version of the Art Nouveau wave that was sweeping Europe. His controversial Secession Building, incorporating elements of an Egyptian tomb, was crowned with an open-work golden orb of laurel leaves, which some Viennese called "the golden cabbage". The artist Klimt designed the metal doors on this building where exhibitions of the new Jugendstil art were shown. We were pleased to read that the organizers of these exhibits had admired the work of William Morris and the Arts and Crafts movements and had invited Mackintosh to participate in the Eighth Vienna Secession Exhibition in 1900. We set out to find other examples of Jugendstil in the city.

Eventually we found a special coffee house suited to one of our current interests, antique kitchenware. *Café Alte Backstube* was a small café-museum housed on the site of a seventeenth century bakehouse. A collection of wooden bread-kneading bowls, carved boards for imprinting the springerle cookies, bakers' crimping wheels and dough scrapers were arranged around the original kilns. We correctly judged that this would be the place to sample an authentic apple strudel.

Demel floats above the other cafés in a class of its own. Its clientele lists emperors, presidents and premiers (John Fitzgerald Kennedy and Nikita Kruschev), who expect the impeccable service and delicacies that set the standard by which others are judged. In several large kitchens pastry chefs work with only the finest pure ingredients to fill the salons with freshly baked *Torten* every morning. In a Regency mirrored room that reflects quiet refinement, glass cases of petit fours, glazed pineapple

Imposing statues, formal gardens and the monumental architecture of the Imperial Natural History Museum is repeated around the *Ringstrasse.*

The Vienna Woods on the way to Salzburg.

tarts and hazlenut cream tortes, pristine on their footed cake stands, wait to be served *mit schlag*, heavy whipped cream. A favourite was *Ischlertorte*, chocolate cake with cherry and almond filling. It is a two hundred year old business which has never compromised on quality.

Café society was raised to an art form at the *Hotel Sacher* when the pastry chef introduced the *Sachertorte*, layers of dark chocolate cake sandwiched with apricot jam and covered with chocolate icing. Located immediately behind the Opera House, the ceiling of this glittering restaurant drips with crystal chandeliers. An orchestra in period dress plays Mozart to theatre-goers seated at white linen-covered tables. The composers still play to an impressive crowd in this city of the waltz.

VIENNESE COUPE

There is little point in my working up a recipe for cakes served in Vienna's famous cafés. They are all available in classic pastry and dessert books, if you have the energy to make them. Instead, try serving an elegant coupe based on the ingredients pastry chefs use for their confections. The amounts will be determined by the number of guests. Get out your best cut-glass or silver dessert dishes. This presentation is all about style, like the city itself.

INGREDIENTS
3 round boulles of rich vanilla ice cream for each guest
a silver pot of strong espresso coffee
a crystal bowl of stiffly whipped cream
a compote of pitted dark cherries soaked in Kirsch
a small bowl of slivered toasted almonds
a block of the best dark chocolate

METHOD
1. Arrange all of the toppings on the table, set with spoons and demitasse cups, before you bring the ice cream from the refrigerator.
2. Explain that guests may chose to include a sample of each, starting with a small demitasse of coffee poured over the ice cream. Or drink it on the side from their cup as preferred.
3. Serve each person a dish of ice cream. Suggest a spoonful of whipped cream (mit schlag) on top.
4. Cherries in liqueur come next, followed by a sprinkling of almonds and a shaving of chocolate. Use a coarse cheese grater or rotary drum grater.

Cold reality faced us in the morning light. The *inside* of the van was covered in frost when we awoke. I lay admiring its delicate tracery on the clay water jug, thinking of sunny Spain and wondering how I would make it to the washrooms. After a thawing breakfast, we decided that a business day would kick-start the circulation. At the American Express office, we filled our shopping bag with mail then carried it to the nearest coffee house. Everyone in Canada was lyrical about an early warm spring. To lift the slight feeling of depression, I went shopping. On the way to Vienna, we had stopped in a town called *Freisach*, where I had asked the proprietor of a small paper shop if he carried scraps, lithographed cutouts that had reached the apex of their form in Austria and Germany in the last century. He gave me the address of *Witte House* in Vienna, which turned out to be a paper paradise. Multi-coloured garlands for every major festival were strung across the ceiling. Huge *papier maché* masks and paper costumes hung on the walls. The shelves bent under the weight of game books, cutouts, cards and pictures. The attendant placed a carton of scrap pages on the counter for me to rifle through. I bought eighteen pages, all reproduced from early designs, which doubled my collection in one swoop. Then I remembered that the next day was Easter Sunday, so I got a giant cardboard egg to fill with treats.

April 6, 1969 EASTER

This day of resurrection brought warm sun and special significance to us. Over an Alpine breakfast of granola and cream, we rejoiced in lives that had been spared and renewed on several levels over the last few months. The discovery of chocolate marzipan eggs and bunnies hiding in the big paper egg occupied the next hour. But the nagging feeling persisted that the significance of the day called for something more than chocolates, good as they were. We set off toward the spire soaring out of the centre of the city. St. Stephen's Gothic Cathedral symbolizes the religious heart of Vienna, the perfect venue in which to appreciate the celebratory music of the holiday. Full throttle organ, angelic choir and rousing *hallelujahs* did the trick.

All music in Vienna leads to thoughts of the River Danube which embraces the city in its curve. Just as we arrived at the banks of the canal, a pleasure cruiser docked. We climbed aboard for a two hour cruise through the lock system, out into the river. The Easter sun warmed us as we sat on the outdoor back benches where we could watch the Viennese walking their Dachshunds along the banks. The water was not blue.

So far, Austria's highlight food experience had been the wonderful hefty brown breads which the bakers sold by weight. And the knockwurst. But we knew that this part of the country had a reputation for more ambitious dishes. On our last evening in Vienna, we got dressed up and treated ourselves to dinner at *Griechenbeisel*, a fifteenth century inn, with ivy dripping around its carved stone arches, waving in front of the small honeycomb-paned windows and trailing down over the door that we entered. A large carving of a kilted bagpiper was lit by an arc lamp over the door. Inside, low vaulted ceilings, yellowed stucco above dark panelling, created an intimate atmosphere. We were seated on walnut bentwood chairs at a table for two, covered in brown and white checked linen. Another figure of a bagpiper, this one in lederhosen, set in a small niche beside our table, roused our curiosity. We asked our waiter (a student eager to try out his English) for an explanation.

"He represents a survivor of the great plague of 1679, a strolling musician who fell into a pit of the dead plague victims and drew attention to his plight by playing the bagpipes. Since then, many more renowned musicians, Mozart, Beethoven, have enjoyed meals here." Like the atmosphere, the fare was not subtle; adequate, but not definitive. We worked our way through broth with chunks of liver paté floating in it, *Wiener Schnitzel* and bean salad. The half flagon of beer came with a creamy head on top, but the coffee came cold. Or maybe we had just been distracted by the strolling zither players.

It should be noted that Viennese restaurants have moved into the twenty-first century. The type of meal we considered typical is rarely served in upscale places now. They are turning to the preferred international light fare; fresh, local ingredients prepared innovatively.

April 9, 1969 SALZBURG

The *autobahn* that connects Vienna with Salzburg follows a mythic route through the Vienna Woods, then flows suspended between sloping pastures and rugged mountains. To the north lay a patchwork of woodlots, farmyards, yellow and brown fields, a lumpy bedspread over the terrain. Quiet roads led down to toy villages, each with its red-domed church. On the south, blurred under a glaring sun, rose the jagged peaks of the Austrian Alps, one brute rearing haughtily into the greyish-white haze. We spread a blanket on the lush grass of the northern landscape and let a brisk wind blow over us as we lunched staring down on a very peaceful pastoral scene. It changed quickly as the pastures gave way to pine forests; the scent of resin filled the cool air as we wove our way between icy blue lakes and waited for Maria to appear with a group of children chanting *doh, a deer, a female deer*.

Mozart took this same route frequently, between Vienna where he composed his master-pieces and Salzburg, where he had been born and baptised in the Salzburg Cathedral. In 2006, both cities were primed to celebrate the 250th anniversary of the composer's birth. In concert halls, parks and stadiums throughout Vienna, every one of Mozart's 626 works will get an airing. To tie this musical extravaganza to the kitchen, a cookbook is to be issued, *Wolfgang is Fat* and *in Good Health*, an historically accurate look at his eating habits in spite of the politically incorrect title.

If your interest is musical and you find yourself in Salzburg, you can rush around to the attractive shrines to his memory that dot the city. As prospective shop-owners, our interest lay on the *Getreidegasse*, a pedestrian street that allows you to walk safely while gazing up to study the swinging gallery of ornate shop signs. The merchants signify their trades with delicate works of the ironmongers' art. Gilded shapes that designate their merchandise - a clock, a boot, a harp, shine amidst intricate black iron scrollwork. These shingles were echoed for us a few months later when we found a book back in London, *Engravings of Trades and Professions*, two of which we commissioned a Canadian art student to reproduce as our store signs.

The camping grounds in Salzburg were in the fields next to a school facing the *Hohensalzburg*, a hill fortress, set on the *Monchsberg* mountain ridge that dominates the city. All the significant peaks, shining in the early morning sun, filled the van windshield. Although it was only 8:30 am, the children's bicycles were lined along the school wall. They had walked past the van so quietly that they had not wakened us. A neighbourhood baker sold us a loaf of malty brown bread for breakfast, still warm from his ovens. A walk along the *Salzbach River* brought us to the *Altstadt*, or Old Town, an entire centre of stunning seventeenth and eighteenth century baroque architecture. Its completeness makes it an anomaly in a world that has lost so much to the ravages of war and urban development. The walk back to camp passed through town squares filled with the encouraging glow of daffodils and the Gardens of the Mirabell Palace below the Castle. As we sat in the van nibbling a Maria -Theresa torte, I thought I heard the Von Trapp family singers, but it was only the voices of our school children, singing very well in unison, in their classroom.

The province of Tyrol had a Grimm's Fairy Tale quaintness due to the yellow stuccoed houses with intricately carved balconies, stencilled window surrounds, and piles of timber stacked neatly up the sides of the walls. Cows dotted pastures that were starred with wildflowers. Every second car had skis attached to the roof heading for the trails that led up from the valley of the Inn River. In a roadside stand set beside a stream so clear you could count the grey pebbles on its bed, a woman was selling freshly grilled trout. Her three small children in pinafores and kerchiefs were gathering armfuls of the blue and yellow flowers that grew wild along the roadside. I am sure that they had posed for one of my scrap sheets purchased in Vienna.

Salzburg Cathedral, where Mozart was baptized, as seen from the *Hohensalzburg*, a hill fortress that dominates the city.

April 11, 1969   INNSBRUCK

We went around in circles trying to find the camping grounds in Innsbruck until we realized that we were on the Brenner Pass heading through the Alps to Italy. A timely route correction brought us to a scenic park of pale willows, tucked under a mountain range where we pulled in beside a Dutch camping couple who made us happy right away with a bag of English paperback books. The four of us took a pot of coffee out to the picnic bench beside a statue of *Walther von der Vogelweide*, a medieval minstrel who stands complete with harp and surrounded by bird-feeding stations. They told us to pause as we walked across the bridge leading into the centre of the town, so that we could take in the pine trees bending over the river Inn and the circle of snow-capped mountains around us. There is no ignoring the Alps in Innsbruck. They bear down on the town as though a hole had been blasted out of their core and the town had been dropped into it.

Once in the centre we needed no prompting to admire the one-of-a-kind architecture. The Golden Roof, with its late-Gothic bay window encrusted with thousands of gold-plated tiles had been built under Emperor Maximilian to provide a royal box for watching entertainments and tournaments in the square below. The Helbing house resembled a large white and pink frosted birthday cake, encrusted with busts, masks and shells, the result of 1500s rococo gone mad. You would be hard-pressed to find a more dramatic main street than the *Marie-Theresa Strasse*. A statue of the Madonna with a halo of stars, stands in the middle of the street, holding the moon, against the backdrop of Innsbruck's ski slopes.

Back in the van with a cup of hot chocolate in hand, we checked out

Van parked in a campsite below the Alps in Innsbruck.

A rude awakening on the Arlberg Pass, Blundenz, near Liechtenstein.

the skiers through a pair of binoculars, as they whizzed down the glaciers facing us. They seemed to be having such a good time on the sun-lit trails, that we considered taking a ride up the slopes the next day. We woke to find the scene obliterated by blizzard conditions and our Dutch neighbours at the van door with the news that the cable car we had counted on taking us to the summit had ripped its side off on a passing post. It was time to try to find spring somewhere else, as it definitely was not in Austria.

As we crossed the 6,000 foot Arlberg Pass, everything was completely blanked out by an impenetrable white curtain. Steam seemed to be rising from the highway until I realized that we were driving through whisps of cloud. Once on the other side, we entered a serious storm. By the time we reached a campsite in *Blundenz*, we had to edge under a canopy of trees whose snow-laden branches arched down to meet the drifts on the ground. My inclusion of a fur-trimmed coat was finally vindicated. We dug it out from the back of the crammed van cupboard and took a country hike that brought back memories of Decembers in Canada, except that here there were forsythia blossoms peeking through the white branches and tulips quivering under a foot of snow. As we hunkered down for an interesting night in our sleeping bags, conditions grew worse. The temperature fell as big, soft flakes cut us off from the outside world.

Neither one of us wanted to shatter the cocoon of body warmth to make the necessary run to the ablution hut in the morning. But David had cleverly attached a string to the interior heater in the van with a loop on the end that he placed under the bedding. He slipped the loop around his big toe and pulled on the heater. Scott of Antarctica would have approved of his self-preservation skills. There was still the ice to chip off the door locks before we could make the dash to the toilets.

SWITZERLAND
Mountains and Chocolate

April 15, 1969   LUCERNE

A December landscape dogged us out of Austria, through Liecht-enstein and across the top of Switzerland, a small nation with colossal peaks. The weather gods were in a dither. Lilac blossoms were encased in ice; bunches of yellow and purple primula were shivering under a sleety blanket. On the descent into the region of the Swiss lakes, the grass became green again and the daffodils waved happy snow-free heads. Mountain wild flowers scented the air that blew in through the van windows with the clanging of cow bells. We pitched camp behind the Lido on Lake Lucerne, where we could watch the paddlewheel steamers ply back and forth in front of a backdrop of the soaring peaks Turner had painted in the moonlight more than a century earlier. One of these boats would take us into the town of Lucerne, ideally situated at the mouth of the Reuss River and this glacier-fed lake.

The town centre is dominated by the *Kapellbrucke*, a fourteenth cen-tury covered bridge which crosses the Reuss River diagonally. The day we first saw it, the entire roof was covered in snow, but even more sig-nificant, the pedestrians crossing the bridge had their eyes focused on the interior of the beamed roof. A series of more than one hundred sev-enteenth century paintings depicting Swiss history were framed in the triangular roof partitions.They had been donated by the leading mer-chants, bankers and governing families of the city and acted as an in-spiring testament to civic pride and an ongoing lesson in local history.

Sadly, a fire in 1993 destroyed two thirds of the original paintings, but the city officials immediately commissioned replicas to be installed in the renovated bridge they held so dear. The large octagonal water tower standing to one side, is a reminder that this bridge was once part of the city's fortifications, an explanation for its peculiar angular position on the river.

The *Kapellgasse*, a narrow brick-paved shopping street, was closed to traffic, allowing pedestrians peace and leisure to appreciate the shop-keepers' window displays. One meat store was a showcase of the butcher's art: rectangular white porcelain platters of prepared shish ke-babs, breaded schnitzels ready for the frypan, rounds of entrecôte wrapped in bacon, a dizzying assortment of sliced hams, bolognas, salamis, wursts and pepperoni. Next door, the bakeshop, in addition to the usual selection of sweet treats, offered *Luzern torten*, large chocolate confections. Each region that we had visited had contributed its own unique culinary temptations to the development of our uninformed but eager palates. The department stores had a comprehensive selection of European merchandise. British goods I had priced in London were no more expensive here. The Cambridge economics student camped next to us tried to explain the influence that the European Free Trade Agreement had on pricing, but when he failed to see a glimmer of understanding, we switched to a discussion of cricket scores.

On a near perfect sunny day we followed the quay built along the lakefront park all the way into Lucerne. For over a century, it has been a popular promenade for the townsfolk; rarely could it have been more beautiful. The air was so clear that every peak fringing the lake was completely visible for the first time, so we sat often on the quiet benches surrounded by spring flowers to soak in the scene. Just past the hotel with the pretty painted facade, David found an antiquarian bookstore. He has a real talent for this kind of thing. We bought a bound volume of the Bazaar magazine for 1867, containing all of the weekly issues of this famous fashion publication. The elderly owner who sold it to us for the

Valleys between the mountains provide transport corridors.

The Kapellbrucke, a 14th century covered bridge across
the Reusse River in Lucerne.

equivalent of $5 had framed several individual prints of the same era and stuck a price tag of $7 on each of them. This book contained hundreds of frameable possibilities that instantly had me filling the walls of a phantom print store.

The next day was just too sad. Another three inches of snow fell on this Swiss idyl, burying our spring hopes along with the poor blossoms. We ran up the campers' white flag of surrender on the van aerial and retreated to one of the camp ground's rental bungalows. Good fortune had directed us to the one site so far that offered this type of alternative accommodation just when we needed it most. Within fifteen minutes, we had moved our necessities from a cold, cramped van to a cheery little chalet in time for breakfast. It was tastefully decorated with a brick floor, chintz curtains and an original oil painting hanging between two real beds. The walls and furnishings were all natural pine, giving the little space a forestry scent. For the first time in months, we were able to pull on clothes while standing up; to cook and wash without being bent over. We began to realize our folly at not having ordered the pop-up roof option with the van.

We decided to act like tourists and pay a visit to the Glacier Gardens, a unique natural monument, witness to the changes caused by the Ice Age to this part of the globe. A path fenced off by rustic railings, takes you around glacial pot holes, formed by water whirling around at the foot of great waterfalls cascading down through crevasses in the ice. A museum on site recreates the atmosphere of a Swiss inn with parquet floors, mullioned windows and intricately carved beams. Old Lucerne is depicted in paintings, prints, porcelain and furnishings. Large open cupboards and armoires are piled with copper and pewter utensils, a concept that stayed with me. Outside, the path continues up past ponds to a colony of marmottes, an alpine animal similar to our groundhog. One of the boys, out for a feed after his long winter's sleep, sat on his haunches with his front paws clasped, yellow teeth quivering for the carrots the keeper fetched.

Further up, you come to a small primative Swiss cottage, austere in all but the magnificent view. A wooden look-out tower at the top offers a panoramic view of Lucerne. Below the Glacier Garden is the Lion Monument, carved into a forty foot niche in a solid wall of rock rising from a still pond. *The Lion of Luzern* is dedicated to the memory of the heroic struggle and final defeat of the Swiss Guards at the hands of a mob in the Tuilleries Garden in Paris, at the time of the French Revolution, 1792. Even though his heart is pierced by a lance, the lion still holds its protective paw over the shield with the lily coat of arms, emblem of the Bourbon kings.

The storm locked us into our snuggery for the better part of a week, but we made good use of the time. I started a "store ideas" notebook listing the matting and framing of fashion prints, gift cards from the antique scrap sheets, possible names for the business, and signage suggestions. Nothing would make a million, but everything would make a difference. We awoke in a warm room and enjoyed a long breakfast at proper table and chairs. Over the second cup of coffee we thought up store window displays. Almost a year of seasonal ideas were sketched out by the third week of April when we realized that it was time to move north out of Switzerland through Zurich to Basel.

April 22, 1969   ZURICH

When you walk down the *Bahnhofstrasse*, Zurich's Fifth Avenue of luxury goods, you are literally walking a few feet above mountains of gold buried in vaults under its sidewalks. This international capital of finance had our heads pivoting at the elegant store displays of diamond and gold Swiss watches, Italian leather goods, and exclusive French couture. We would have to revise our amateur sketches in the spiral notebook. The nearby American Express office was located above a small restaurant called *The Parade*. We collected a bag full of mail and took it downstairs to this bright, efficient, cheerily modern room to digest the news with a pleasant lunch. Over a hearty plate of chicken broth we opened the envelop that contained David's grant acceptance for his post grad work. During the poached trout and boiled potatoes, I found out that citizenship papers were required before mine could come through. My heart was not in this paper chase. With the endive salad, we rearranged our future. Instead of trying to juggle two careers, I would be a fulltime store owner. David would still lead a divided life until we got the business on its feet. It felt good to have settled everything over a one dollar lunch.

Zurich was the ideal place to make sound financial decisions. The Romans set up customs houses here, establishing the city's fiscal supremacy early in its history. Workers' guilds edged out the nobility to become the ruling class as early as the fourteenth century. While we sat in a city where rules, ledgers, order and stability reigned, my paper work had been found faulty. Yet James Joyce had written significant chunks of *Ulysses* in this centre of commerce. It had been home for other writers and intellectuals, like Jung and Lenin for a time. That unstructured art form, dadaism, had sprung up in this staid town. There was no doubt, that this was the spot to make the break from a traditional career into a riskier business.

After lunch we headed for the older section of the city called *Niederdorf* to investigate *Dorfli*, a narrow pedestrian's shopping street of Gothic buildings housing delis and confectioners that introduced us to some Swiss specialties. Their signature foods, chocolate and cheese, both use milk from the cows that pasture on the sides of the mountains. Both are staple foods for those who climb or ski. A chocolate bar is packed into every climber's knapsack for energy when it is needed most. *Toblerone* is even shaped like the famous Matterhorn. Emmental, the cheese with the holes, is made in the Emme Valley. We saw wheels of this famous cheese 45 inches wide, weighing up to 200 pounds. Gruyère is a denser cheese with a taste that reminds me of mushrooms. Both of them owe their unique flavours to the tasty diet of alpine herbs that the cows munch. A combination of these cheeses is used to make fondue, a warm, sustaining melt spiked with Kirsch, which is perfect fare in a chalet. When we ordered one in a restaurant at the foot of a ski run, it came in the traditional side-handled orange fondue pot set on an alcohol table-burner. Long, spiked forks were stuck in the basket of cubed bread. David made a drawing of this equipment which we used on recipe cards to include with our future sales of fondue pots. Whenever salesmen in Canada of the seventies asked me, "How long do you think this fondue craze will last?" it was a dead giveaway that they had never been in Switzerland, where this meal has been sustaining mountain folk for centuries.

SWISS CHEESE FONDUE

A flameproof earthenware or enamelled cast iron pot , a stirring stick and a safe stand for holding the fuel are essential for cheese fonduing. The thick earthenware is a slow, even heat conductor, less likely to scorch melting cheese than metal. A chafing dish with a water pan works well. If you have a fire-proof pot, you can do the preparation on the stove. Otherwise, over a fondue burner will be safer but slower.

INGREDIENTS

1/2 pound of Emmental provides a delicate, sweet flavour
1/2 pound of Gruyère gives a stronger, nuttier flavour
1 tablespoon cornstarch
1 clove of garlic cut in half
2 cups dry white wine
3 tablespoons Kirsch (cherry brandy)
a pinch (an eighth of a teaspoon) of cayenne
a scraping of fresh nutmeg
a loaf of crusty bread, cut into cubes
boiled potatoes, cut into one inch cubes
slices of crisp apples

METHOD

1. Grate the cheese and toss in the cornstarch to coat.
2. Rub the sides of the pot with the garlic.
3. Bring the wine to a simmer.
4. Add the cheese by handfuls, stirring well with a wooden spoon to incorporate each addition.

5. Stir in the Kirsch.
6. Add the seasonings.
7. Keep more wine handy to thin the mixture should it become too thick. If the fondue is too thin, make a paste of a little more corn-starch mixed with a spoon or two of Kirsch and stir it in.
8. In addition to dipping bread and potatoes, try wedges of crisp apple.
9. Serve at the table in a proper fondue pot on a stand which holds fondue fuel safely. Control the heat.

Swiss restaurants often offer a few special treats. When you reach the bottom scrapings in the pot, the waiter might bring a fresh egg to your table to break into the residue of crusty cheese. Stir and enjoy. Each person might also receive a small glass of Kirsch in which you dip the bread cube before covering it in cheese.

SWISS CHOCOLATE FONDUE

A chocolate fondue is an easy and convivial way to end a meal or spend a winter evening by the fire. A smaller earthenware pot is called for. They are available set on stands with a candle underneath. The chocolate can be melted on the stove in a double boiler to prevent scorching then transferred to a table-top dish warmed by a candle. Smaller forks and dessert plates are needed.

Buy the best quality blocks of chocolate that you can afford from a specialty chocolate shop.

INGREDIENTS
6 ounces bitter chocolate
7 ounces semi-sweet chocolate
1/2 cup heavy cream
3 tablespoons Cognac
1 teaspoon vanilla
fresh cherries
strawberries
seedless grapes
pieces of pineapple
pound cake cut into squares or fingers

METHOD
1. Warm the cream in a small saucepan.
2. Break the chocolate into small pieces and place in the top of a double boiler, which is on the stove with hot water in the bottom section.

3. Pour the heated cream over the chocolate and stir until melted.
4. Add liqueur - could be fruit based such as Grand Marnier, if you do not have Cognac on hand.

   This is a perfect opportunity to use a miniature bottle.
5. Transfer the fondue to a table-top warming dish.
6. Arrange the fruits and cake on an attractive platter with the pot of chocolate placed in the centre for dipping.

One of the nicest touches in public buildings here (duly noted in my spiral book), was their liberal use of fresh flowers. The Cathedral in Lucerne had huge branches of white blossoms in pots set in front of the black iron choir screen and crucifix. Large earthen vases of tulips and daffodils, a single rose in a heavy glass bottle, or clay pots of hyacinths stood beside the cash register in shops. In the centre of each white linen tablecloth at *The Parade* where we had lunched, stood a silver trumpet-shaped vase holding a tulip and a sprig of pink blossoms from an apple tree. Even a budget restaurant could be elegant. Jardinières stuffed with flowers stood in front of one of the wrought iron gates enclosing a serious financial institution. On the way back to camp, I picked some white wildflowers to put in our Brolio bottle. A touch of spring in the van and the beginning of a lifetime habit.

The Eighth Country on the 1969 Odyssey

GERMANY
Beer and Castles

April 23, 1969 FREIBURG in BREISGAU

David persisted in trying to find the *Badische Weinstrasse*, the scenic wine route up the valley to Freiburg, and I'm very pleased that he succeeded. It turned out to be a funny little road, deserted for the autobahn, tumbling over hills planted with vines and weaving through ageless rural villages of Hansel and Gretel cottages. Spring wildflowers dotted the hillocks on each side of this enchanted road, where mystery lurked around each bend and over each hill. Looming on all sides were the ominous pine slopes of the Black Forest, wreathed with melancholy shrouds of rain clouds. The fresh scent of resin on the cool air stimulated our taste buds as I passed along some facts of the region to David. "The Black Forest is noted for certain culinary specialties. The name has been given to Black Forest Ham and Black Forest Cake." We stopped at the next village and had a deli fill a crusty bun with the ham then moved along to a pastry shop for the gateau. These thin layers of dark chocolate cake spread with liquer-soaked cherry conserve, became the standard dessert offering in North American "continental" restaurants in the 1970s. I never did re-order it subsequent to that first taste, afraid of disappointment.

Freiburg has every reason to be a happy city. Nestled at the entrance to the forest and the wine country, it has been a university town since the mid-fifteenth century, with a student population that no doubt still helps to support the smart boutiques lining its main street. A red brick, triple-arched clock tower spans this street, connecting the enclosed arcades on each side of the road that offer weather and traffic protection to the shopper. Then there is the maze of narrow cobbled lanes and the oldest inn in Germany, The Red Bear, under the sign of a golden bear swinging atop an ornate iron shingle. But the show-stopper is the fine Gothic Minster with a soaring spire that towers over the town pulling you toward the cathedral square. The red stone of the region has been chiselled as finely as lace on the exterior of this medieval building. We approached it on a Saturday morning when it was encircled by a busy jumble of red and white awnings covering fruit carts, flower stalls, and sausage wagons. Townsfolk juggled for red cabbages and sacks of onions in front of the Renaissance colonnade of the historic Merchants' Hall. With residual memories of English cathedral closes, David sniffed out an antiquarian book and print shop nearby which had a terrific collection of art reproductions, postcards, engravings, and botanical prints. I bought a series, *La Belle Jardinière*, a nostalgic depiction of a turn-of-the-century lady shown at her varied garden tasks in each month of the year. Her life seemed so serenely ordered.

The patches of garden attached to the small farms we passed on the *Weinstrasse* brought this series of prints to life. Small, brilliant clumps of yellow and purple primula tucked along the side of a stone barn, indicated that a gardening spirit hovered here. These farm towns seemed to have been unpacked from the net bags we used to get at Christmas, containing miniature wooden haywagons, chickens, pigs and square brick houses. In the vineyard villages and towns that we drove through, such as *Durbach* and *Oberkirch*, the wine production added an interesting dimension. From our narrow road, we could see into large wine cellars where huge barrels and racks of bottles were awaiting the annual *Volksfest* in September. Since we would not be here then, we detoured to sample some of the most impressive wines produced a little further west - *Sylvaner* and *Gewurztraminer*. Pocket-sized villages yield noble vintages.

Just past the outskirts of *Baden-Baden*, the road wound up into the almost dark reaches of this pine forest. The gables of high altitude hotels, which had made this thermal spa renowned, appeared through occasional breaks in the trees. It was another example of a good place which the Romans had discovered first.

Evenings became more pleasureable once we drove within the broadcasting beam of Radio Luxembourg. Their programming appealed to the caravan of youth that was drifting across the continent. The Beatles, The Who and The Stones performed as we sat at the small pop-up table making lists of possible names for a phantom store. We narrowed it down to *Cabbages and Kings*, partly because we thought that Lewis Carroll's verse from *The Walrus and the Carpenter*, summarized the moment:

> *The time has come, the Walrus said,*
> *To speak of many things,*
> *Of ships and seas and sealing wax,*
> *And Cabbages and Kings.*

Mainly because the phrase covered kitchenwares as well as the more noble Victoriana which we intended to sell at first until we made contact with suppliers of European cookware.

One night as Frankie belted out "*I Did It My Way*" on Radio Lux, David drew our opening flier inspired by the illustrations on the menu given to us in The Cock Tavern months ago in London. At the top of the page was a fat leafy cabbage, crowned like a king. Flowing from him, down either side of the page, came a procession of candlesticks, egg whisks, books, Staffordshire dogs, soup tureens and a rope of garlic. The centre of the page was blank, waiting to be filled in with our location and mission statement.

April 25, 1969 HEIDELBERG

From our campsite at the brink of the swollen Neckar River, we watched a seemingly endless file of barges float past. A handful of passengers at the railing of a pleasure steamer waved to us on their way through the wooded hills towards Worms. David started to keep a boat tally with a pile of pebbles as counters. When he got up to thirty we remembered that his father had asked us to drink his health at the Schloss in Heidelberg. We roused ourselves from the river bank for a hike into town.

A walk along the *Hauptstrasse*, a long traffic-free High Street of quality businesses, took us past the fourteenth-century University area of *The Student Prince*, Sigmund Romberg's light opera that encouraged us to "drink, drink, drink". Heading the food favourites here is the holy trinity of *bier, brot mit wurst*. The beer and the sausage made good partners, but the bread could stand alone. One bakery window near the *Fischmarkt* was filled with oval sourdoughs, ridged wheels of dark rye, loaves of crunchy sunflower bread, and woven baskets piled with seeded rolls. The variety of breads we met on the continent was one of the most pleasurable aspects of the trip. But the German bread topped them all for flavour and texture. It could be a meal in itself. Our present farmers' markets in southwestern Ontario, have German immigrants who supply us with breads of this quality from their brick ovens. Our local farmers also produce some excellent wursts from their livestock. This is one food memory we can re-live regularly.

BIER, BROT, MIT WURST

I add beer to this cabbage and sausage casserole and eat it with a good German rye bread to complete the trinity.

INGREDIENTS

1 pound coil of fat garlic sausage (*Wurst*)
2 tablespoons vegetable oil - canola or sunflower or grapeseed
1 medium Spanish onion, peeled and thinly sliced in whole rounds
2-1/2 cups shredded Savoy cabbage
1 apple - peeled, cored and sliced to equal 2 cups
1/2 cup pale beer (*Bier*)
2 large slices of light rye bread (*Brot*)
1 teaspoon herbal salt (coarse salt with dried herbs such as savory)
1 tablespoon Dijon mustard

METHOD
1. Warm the oil in a large, heavy skillet which has a lid.
2. Toss the onion rings in the oil until separated and softened. Do not allow to brown.
3. Remove onions to a plate while you brown the sausage in this skillet.
4. Cut the coil into 12 two inch logs. There should be enough oil left to brown them on all sides.
5. Add the onions back into the pan.
6. Cook together for about 5 minutes.
7. Cut the cabbage into 4 wedges. Remove the hard white core.
8. This recipe needs just one of the quarters. Wrap the rest to reserve

for a slaw salad or cabbage and potatoes.

9. Cut the wedge in half lengthwise, then shred crosswise into thin slices. It should equal about 2-1/2 cups of cabbage. Spread it over the contents of the skillet. Sprinkle with salt and savory.

10. Pour the beer over the cabbage. Cover the pan and simmer on low heat for 15 minutes.

11. Spread the apple slices evenly over the top. Cover and simmer a further 15 minutes.

12. Test a piece of the sausage to make sure it is no longer pink. Continue on simmer until done.

13. You may stir some of the mustard into the liquid in the pan or serve it on the side *mit Brot.*

On the way to the *Kornmarkt*, we passed several book and paper stores. When I asked for scrap sheets in one of them to add to my collection, the owner smiled and said, "*Ah, Rosenbilder*". At least that's what it sounded like. He did produce some fine examples of rosy-cheeked children in aprons and kerchiefs hugging bunches of flowers or carrying *kugelhopf* cakes. One of these scraps decorated the opening sign for our store the following August.

On to Heidelberg Castle, up the steep brick road, overhung with new-leafed trees and ivy-covered houses. Perched high above the city, in a woodland setting, this ancient *Schloss* still retains parts from the original red stone fortress and subsequent additions, dating from the thirteenth century, a romantic ruin that has inspired poets and novelists. Baroque banqueting halls and reception rooms have been added over the centuries to form a massive complex, parts of which are still used for concerts and special events. We arrived on the terrace in the middle of one of them - a U.S. military wedding was in progress, full dress uniform, crossed swords and all. I wonder what the past forty years of married life have brought to this bride and groom on whom the sun shone at the top of Heidelberg that happy day. We joined the wedding guests at the ramparts gazing down on the medieval red brick roofs, the bridges over the River Neckar, and the woods beyond. When one of them told me about a sixteenth century wine cellar we could visit at the west end of the terrace, we hurried over to that wing of the castle to see one of the largest wine vats in the world, the *Heidelberg Tun*, an impressive gleaming wooden barrel that can hold over 200,000 litres of wine. It seemed like an ideal spot to drink to Reverend Lindsay's health by raising a frosty stein accompanied by a platter of thinly sliced sausages of the region.

Before two World Wars frosted their cordial relationship, the English sent teenage sons and daughters to Heidelberg private tutoring schools for language and history instruction. Like visitors through the ages, they returned home with an urge to bake. We can thank the pastry shops of Heidelberg for inspiring Mrs. Isabella Beeton when she attended school in this town in the 1850s. Kathryn Hughes' excellent biography, *The Short Life and Long Times* of Mrs. Beeton, explains the significance of the German acceptance of domestic skills as one of the feminine arts.

Heavy rain pounding the roof of the van, woke us the next morning. When I looked through the crack in the curtains covering our windshield, there was a fishing derby in full swing a few yards away, oblivious to the deluge. The anglers were getting soaked but feeling no pain. We pulled up stakes and headed for Worms, the city on the Rhine, where by decree of a council in 1521, Martin Luther was declared a heretic and sent into exile.

In spite of Luther's stand against Rome, the bells of the cathedral in Worms were rallying the faithful when we arrived in time for service on that miserable morning. We sat out the storm in a café before continuing on to Mainz, home to another man who changed the course of civilization, Johannes Gutenberg. During the 1999 preparations for world-wide millennium celebrations, lists of the most significant contributors to our culture were compiled and voted upon. Gutenberg was proclaimed the winner, for without his invention of moveable type setting, none of our global literacy or the proliferation of Luther's *Ninety-Five Theses*, nailed to the door of *Wittenberg Cathedral*, would have been possible. We owe our world of books to him.

The *Rheingoldstrasse* followed close to the banks of the Rhine, Germany's oldest road of romance with a castle around every bend, all wreathed with the ghosts of the *Lorelei* , mythical sirens who lured boatmen to the depths. Even here, in this land of castles straight out of our poetry books, commerce had paved the way. The powerful owners of the castles had extorted dues from the trade merchants that plied the Rhine Valley for centuries. The first impressive castle whose turrets rose above the dark green woods, was perched conveniently over a campsite. Once the van was parked facing the river, we began the hike up to Castle

Rheinstein.

A young guide, fluent in both German and English, toured a group of us through the Gothic chambers in which Prince Frederick of Prussia and his Princess had spent their days. His thirteenth-century stone chamber was hung with swords, guns, spikes, and metal helmets. It was no picnic being a ruler on the ramparts of the Rhine. The six foot six Prince had to sleep sitting up in a four foot bed, just on the off-chance that he might have to defend his castle against sudden attack. We remarked that a portrait hanging in the hall bore a resemblance to King George V. The guide explained that one of the Prince's descendants was a cousin of the English king. During two World Wars, blood did not appear to be thicker than water.

The Princess' writing room with its high arched windows overlooking a misty terrain, made me think of Mary Shelley's fascination with Frankenstein Schloss, a ruined castle not far from this spot, that some say turned her imagination towards the darker aspects of creation. She had visited this area in 1814 with the poet Shelley and Claire Clairmont. The setting had so impressed her, that she called up the haunting memories several years later when a lightning storm near Geneva jolted her into writing a classic tale of horror. In spite of this sombre tour, we slept soundly on the banks of the Rhine, undisturbed by nightmares.

A pleasure boat with *Das Rhein* painted on its hull, steamed past the van that morning at about nine o'clock. Just before we reached Bacharach, a wine town as lyrical as its name in the shadow of Stahleck Castle, it was our turn to pass *Das Rhein* as it sat out near an island in the river. Gauging by the steamer, we were making good progress, so we took a walk around this attractive town with its treasured stock of half-timbered buildings. In a small store, we found a pair of carved wooden moulds depicting a medieval king and his queen. They looked a lot like the gingerbread moulds we had seen in Pollock's Toy Shop in London. Sure enough, the owner explained to us that *spekulatius*, a spicy gingerbread dough, was pressed into these forms to imprint it before baking.

We made a note of the recipe and handed it out to our customers years later at holiday times.

It should have come as no surprise that we would discover kitchen treasures deep in the German countryside. Regional specialties often originate in farm kitchens. Yet it was like a gift from the northern sprite they fondly call a "kitchen witch", to come upon a tin fluted tube mould a few hours later, in the medieval town of *Oberwesel*, at a flea market under the turreted slate domes of its castle. It looked like the form used to bake *kugelhopf*, the yeasty cakes found on most bakers' shelves. Studded with almonds and raisins, they are a treat to be shared with family and friends on the birthday of your name saint. In other words, I could have one on the birthday of Saint Anne. Sort of like enjoying two birthday cakes in one year. We have since found beautiful examples of this cake form in white porcelain and brown earthenware. When we had the store, one of our German distributors imported elegant ovenproof glass versions. They all were used to bake *kugelhopfs* on those special saints' days that used to be marked on every family's calendar.

At Koblenz, where the Rhine meets the Moselle, the very name of this river reminded us to stop for a cold glass of wine. The Romans began the cultivation of vines on these slopes, whose slate supplied minerals to fertilize the grapes. The resulting wines have a fruitiness that calls for a special dessert. We were fortunate in our choice of café. The glass of Moselle was frosty and the dessert was a version of what I call tutti-fruiti, a rich compote of plums and cherries soaked in rum. Generally this rich sauce is served over pudding or cream. Ours came on top of a vanilla sponge cake. Many German families treasure their own special recipe, improvised by adding fruits as they become ripe over the seasons, to a large pot of rum. Our shelves in the store always displayed several of these decorative *rumtopfs*, usually blue ceramic, with instructions inside for making your own powerful confection.

RUMTOPF

You will need a covered tall container - glazed stoneware, porcelain or glass - that will hold about six litres. What goes into your rum pot is up to you and seasonal availability. What comes out is a heady concoction of fruits in a sugary liqueur syrup. The pot is brought to the table on festive occasions for the head of the family to dress a sponge cake, ice cream or pudding with a spoonful.

1. Start in May by washing out your rum pot, airing it well and selecting a cool spot in the basement where it will stay.
2. Buy a litre of good white rum.
3. June - as the local strawberries come on the market, select firm, blemish-free fruit. Place the washed, dried and hulled berries on the bottom of the pot. For each pound of fruit sprinkle on 1 cup of sugar that has been stored in a cannister with a vanilla bean pod. Slowly dribble all of the rum down the side of the pot. The berries will absorb the rum and sink. As other fruits are added, you will have to top up with more rum. The liquid should remain one or two inches above the fruit. Keep the pot covered all the time between additions.
4. Buy more rum.
5. July - add pitted cherries, blueberries and more sugar.
6. August - red and black raspberries should be available.
7. Larger fruits with skins - apricots, peaches, plums - need to be blanched, peeled and pitted before being halved.
8. Do not bother with apples, bananas or pears, they go mushy.
9. Buy more rum.

You become increasingly aware of the progress of the season as you watch the market stalls for perfect fruit worthy of inclusion in your rum pot.

When you have added the last fruit, cover the pot and let it stand for several weeks. Check the liquid level. Keep it about two inches above the fruits. Try to keep it covered in a cool spot, 45°F degrees, is almost ideal, but may be a challenge in modern homes. Garage? Cellar?

Resist sampling until the holidays.

We followed the *Rheingoldstrasse* along the Rhine River,
the road of romance with a castle around every bend.

April 28, 1969 COLOGNE

Eight months earlier, while I had stayed in Glasgow with Aunt Esther, David had taken the boat over to Cologne to pick up our van. For lunch, he took me back to the restaurant under the hotel room in which he had spent his bachelor evening last August. He still remembers with a sigh, the fluffy eiderdown that smothered him into noddyland that night. The same waitress, who no doubt had cast that same amorous glance at David, introduced me to *spaetzle*, nodules of dough that were a cross between a malformed noodle and a tiny dumpling. With a little prodding, I discovered that they are essentially a batter of eggs, flour and water forced through a metal device into a simmering broth. Several years later, I located a proper spaetzle maker. It resembles a long, flat grater with a moveable box riding on its sides. The dough that is placed in this box should be the right consistency to ooze through the holes an inch or so into a simmering broth before being cut off by the movement of the top compartment. That evening, ours was served as an accompaniment to roasted veal by the buxom waitress with the heaving breasts.

SPAETZLE MIT SCHNITZEL

Veal escalopes are more difficult to find in our area than pork schnitzels. Two butchers near us offer thinly flattened scallops of pork, breaded and herbed, ready for a fast sauté in butter. They are best accompanied by spaetzle in a sauce.

I did not keep one of the special devices we sold to form these little dumplings, so I improvise with a flat grater with large holes and a stiff spatula to push the dough through.

INGREDIENTS

This makes 4 side servings.

1 large egg at room temperature

1/3 cup half water/half milk mixed (not 1/3 cup of each)

1 cup of all-purpose flour mixed with 1/2 teaspoon salt

SAUCE

1/2 cup finely chopped onion

3 slices bacon

2 teaspoons butter

1/3 cup cubed Emmental cheese

salt and pepper to taste

METHOD

1. Whisk the egg in a measuring cup with the watery milk.
2. Make a well in the centre of the flour and salt in a bowl into which you pour the liquid.
3. Stir until a ball of paste forms. It should not be a stiff dough.

4. Put a pot (that your grater will sit across) on to boil with several quarts of salted water.
5. Meanwhile start the sauce by frying the bacon over low heat to draw out the fat.
6. Remove the slices to drain and cut into small dice.
7. Sauté the chopped onion in the bacon fat combined with the butter.
8. Take the frying pan off the heat while you cook the dumplings in the pot of water.
9. Straddle the grater across the top of the pot of boiling water.
10. Spoon the dough on to the top of the grater about 1/2 cup at a time.
11. Push it back and forth across the grater using a stiff flat-ended spatula. You will develop a rhythm as the batter becomes warm and smooth over the simmering water. Little noodles about an inch long will begin to drop into the water. When they are cooked, they will float to the surface. It takes about 5 minutes.
12. Lift the spaetzle out with a draining spoon and place in the frying pan which has the bacon and onions. Warm gently while incorpoating the cubed Emmental.
13. Season with salt and pepper. Some people like a grating of fresh nutmeg.

Back at the riverside campsite, we watched *Das Rhein* sail by for the third time in one day, finally at the end of its voyage. We bought a packet of fish and chips, of all things, from a portable wagon in the camp, and enjoyed this culinary relapse as a blazing red sunset lit the bridges over the Rhine and the Gothic twin spires of Cologne Cathedral.

The scene wasn't so rosy in front of the cathedral the next day. Virginia Woolf's observations on continental cathedrals (*see Hungry Hearts - England and Spain*) rang all too true. This massive Gothic landmark sat near the station, traffic swirling around it without the buffer of the English green cathedral close. The paved plaza, where painters and buskers now ply their trade, did not yet front its entrance. In spite of a traffic ban on the main thoroughfares, congestion best describes the feeling in the centre of a city that was still reeling from devastating Allied bombings. We were impressed around the old market place, and in other German cities that had suffered war damage, to see reconstructions of the original gabled town houses, churches and civic buildings. These municipalities did not want to cut themselves off from their past. Prince Charles in his book *A Vision of Britain*, bemoans the fact that London lost the opportunity to rebuild on a human scale after the Blitz presented them with a clean slate:

> *What was rebuilt after the war has succeeded in wrecking London's skyline and spoiling the view of St. Paul's in a jostling scrum of skyscrapers, all competing for attention.*

He considers Britain to have fallen for the North American dream of commercial expediency over civic values. Aware that we would be soon sailing back to North America, urban design was much on our minds during our last month in Europe.

BELGIUM
Battlefields and the Baroque

April 29, 1969 BRUSSELS

I had been working my way through *Vanity Fair*, William Thackeray's epic satire on human foibles, ever since the Dutch couple gave it to us in a pile of paperbacks at the Innsbruck campsite. We were now a few miles away from the physical and emotional centre of the book - the site of the Battle of Waterloo, about eleven miles south of Brussels. I was attracted to Thackeray's suggestion that some events behind the scenes of this heroic struggle to determine the fate of Europe might be more interesting than the actual field of conflict. He was almost affirming my penchant for life below stairs. On the night before the battle, he brings the English regimentals and their wives to a glittering ball in Brussels. Indiscretions take place in this gay social setting before death closes in.

We recognized the battle site by the lion commemorative monument sitting on top of a grassy pyramid surrounded by rolls of wheat. The farmhouses and lush fields have domesticated the place where Napoleon lost an empire. This was Thackeray's succinct comment on the momentous event:

> *No more fighting was heard at Brussels - the pursuit rolled miles away. The darkness came down on the field and city, and Amelia was praying for George, who was lying on his face, dead, with a bullet through his heart.*

It is estimated that 47,999 others met their Waterloo with George that day in 1815 on those now peaceful fields.

We camped in a field that night - not a battlefield, a soccer field. It did not seem a wise idea for the city to allow itinerant foreigners in vans to park next to the school playgrounds, but there we were, with municipal blessing. The goal posts framed the windshield. David kept score and I continued to doggedly follow Becky Sharp's adventures as the ball whacked against the side of the van.

The next day it was easy to see Brussels through Becky Sharp's eyes - a gutsy city with handsome features built with a high regard for commerce. Sometimes it had been down on its luck, but it always had the wherewithal to climb back up. It suited Becky because it was essentially a middle class city built by merchants and proud of it. The golden showplace, *Grand-Place*, which Cocteau called "living theatre", was built by the seventeenth century guild houses. This square of Baroque grandeur, each facade topped with different gilt figures, was originally commissioned by butchers, bakers and haberdashers to serve as their halls and

A lion sits on top of a grass pyramid marking the site of
the Battle of Waterloo, eleven miles south of Brussels.

meeting places. Flower markets are now held in the centre, surrounded by chocolate and lace stores and cafés. In 2010 it was voted the most beautiful square in Europe.

It was our misfortune to visit this city in the sixties, when the demolition and building crews were working overtime to erect as many steel and glass towers as possible. My journal bemoans a dull, grey day spent fighting traffic congestion, even in the golden square, and over-reacting to tacky souvenir stores with rows of the little town symbol, *Manneken Pis*, standing ready to urinate in the windows of its heritage buildings. *Vanitas Vanitatum* according to Thackeray fitted my critical mood.

Things improved when the sun bounced off the buildings and warmed our chilled bones on the first of May. The air was perfumed by itinerant flower sellers holding out tight bouquets of lily-of-the-valley on every corner. May Day is celebrated as a holiday across Europe and Brussels put on its Paris dress for the occasion. Chocolate stalls opened onto the sidewalks offering trays of square, triangular and mounded confections filled with liqueurs and nuts.

In a holiday mood, we caught a bus out to the Atomium, the iconic symbol of Expo58, on the site of Brussels' World Fair. We had tea under one of the legs of a billion times magnification of an iron molecule. Escalators connect each of the spheres and a panoramic view is seen from the top.

But on the whole, Brussels is recalled as a missed opportunity. If you have been reading this account without skipping pages, you will have noticed that the revolutionary artistic movement that began in England with William Morris and spread across Europe from 1880 to 1910 under the names *Art Nouveau, Jugendstil* and *Secession Style* has formed a *leitmotiv* on our travels. And here we were in Brussels for three days without realizing that examples of the movement's best decorative objects filled its museums in the *Art Nouveau* buildings lining its streets. Charles Rennie Mackintosh designed a School of Art in Glasgow; Victor Horta gave Brussels the *Maison du Peuple*. Here was an artist who turned a whiplash into the frame for a mirror, the back of a chair, or the railing of a balcony. And we could have walked through Horta's house, filled with his own sinuous furniture, had we known it existed. Another fine example of this style architecture is the Musical Instruments Museum. Masterworks inside and out.

Our biggest lost opportunity was neglecting to visit a warehouse, *Waucquez*, full of light, curvaceous wrought-iron balconies and open spaces, that he designed in 1903 for a textile wholesaler. The building was derelict until the 1980s, when one of *Art Nouveau*'s most passionate supporters, Guy Dessicy, a colourist on the original *Tintin* comic books, directed a two-year restoration to create the Belgian Comic Strip Center. It now houses a world famous collection of comic strips, starring *Tintin*, one of David's favourite characters. He still laments the loss of his boyhood stash of original *Entertaining Comics*, jettisoned in one of the many family moves. Even if you have no interest in this art form, the museum has a beautiful *Art Nouveau* brasserie where you can lunch on *moules et frites*. Brussels merits a return trip.

In the *Grand-Place*, at the centre of the city, a flower stall sits in the middle of a square of gilded buildings, erected in the 17th century by tradesmen's guilds.

The Atomium marks the site of Expo58.

HOLLAND
Bulbs and Bicycles

May 3, 1969 GOUDA

Once we crossed the Belgian border into the Netherlands, we were in a delta region of bridges joining broad flat fields which provide pasture for fat cattle and rich black soil for scarlet tulips. By the time we reached Gouda, after three on a Saturday afternoon, we expected everything to be closed according to European custom. Instead, a carnival gaiety greeted us in the marketplace between the church and the Gothic Town Hall, the pace set by a hurdy-gurdy grinder cranking out cheery tunes on a 1930's stylized nickelodeon. Sales were still brisk at stalls of roasted cashews, smoked fish and flowers. One of the vendors tried to convince us to stay until Thursday. "That's the day we have an open-air cheese market held in front of the Town Hall. Local farmers bring in wheels of our famous Gouda for tasting and selling. At least you can't leave without a wedge today."

Keukenhof Gardens in the first week of May is a
brilliant showplace of Dutch bulbs.

The van got a window box of tulips and daffodils.

CHEESE WITH FRUIT IN CALVADOS

Dried fruit is an ideal camping staple. Especially in Europe, when market stalls display a dizzying array. Since they sold from bulk bins, we could select tasting samples of dried apricots, pears, apples, raisins, figs, prunes. If there was some brandy or fruit liqueur in the van, I'd pour some over mixed fruit in a covered container and serve it with cream or cheese, depending on the stop-of-the-day. This combination was perfect with Gouda cheese.

INGREDIENTS
4 dried figs
1/2 cup dried apple slices
1/4 cup dried apricots
zested peel of half a lemon
3 tablespoons fine granulated sugar
2 tablespoons Calvados
2 tablespoons water
a wedge of Gouda, served at room temperature

METHOD
1. Remove the bits of stem from the figs before quartering them.
2. Cut the apple slices in half.
3. Dice the apricots.
4. Toss fruit together in a saucepan with the lemon zest, sugar and liquids.
5. Simmer until figs are soft.
6. Store in a covered dish until you are ready to serve.
7. On a dessert plate, place a generous slice of Gouda cheese. Mound a spoonful of fruit on the side with a dribble of the sweet syrup.

A ceramicist in this town still made the long, white clay pipes that Dutch men have been smoking for centuries. A year or two later, when I was in the Toronto warehouse of a Dutch importer, he showed me a wooden crate filled with these fragile pipes nestled between layers of straw. We had them shipped to our store simply because we thought them to be an example of a unique and passing icon from another age. Imagine our surprise when they were snapped up within a few days by bearded art students who attended the school near our store. They appreciated them on a more practical level.

May was the best month of the year to be in Holland. On the brief two-mile drive to our campsite, we toured the back canals, passing yachts tied up beside the gardens of thatch-roofed houses, as though they were the family sedan. Because of the flat terrain, bicycles were more common than cars, with mothers and their blond children pedalling in tandem along the miles of canal tow paths or special bike routes. Blue skies, cattle reflected in still waters, red barnyards, white houses with window boxes filled with spring bulbs - pinch me, I'm dreaming.

We must have been parked on a network of roots and sticks or some equally spongy matter, for the van bounced whenever anyone walked past. Although we knew that we were surrounded by narrow waterways on every side, it was still a shock to watch a red sail in the sunset glide by the rear window as we settled down for the night.

As we were leaving the town of *Leiden* near the North Sea, a series of red and yellow signs pointed the way to *Keukenhof Gardens* (Kitchen Gardens) situated on the site of an old estate. We drove dazzled through intense fields of scarlet tulips to park along with several hundred cars on this special viewing Sunday in Holland's world-famous gardens. It just doesn't seem right to be typing this description of seven million bulbs in black and white. *Keukenhof* requires a rainbow alphabet to capture the clusters of snowy white hyacinths called "Blizzard", planted beside the squares of rich blue "Delft". A duck followed by nine newly-hatched yellow chicks, swam around in a pond that was circled by yellow daffodils under cherry trees in blossom. From the top of a windmill at the foot of the garden, you risked retina damage looking out on seven million tulips in full bloom. These seven acres were a canny example of combining pleasure with profit. The displays were a showcase for the country's international bulb trade. Botanists exhibit the latest color combinations in parrot tulips and landscape designers impress the world with their naturalist settings. Even the spent blooms are used to turn a *gilder*. They are cut off each day and formed into huge long garlands, like leis for the visitors' cars. We bought one for the van - a fat string of daffodils and tulips that we tied around the front under the windshield. It was like having a portable window box but it really was the prettiest highway advertising imaginable. Cars in the opposite lane would honk and wave when they saw us coming and probably the woman would nudge the driver and say, "Let's go to the *Keukenhof* dear."

May 5, 1969   AMSTERDAM

The sun beat in through an opening in the plexiglass dome of the waterboat that was taking us around the canals under most of Amsterdam's four hundred bridges. The fresh green buds on the trees had not yet fully opened, so that our view of the houses lining the banks was unimpeded. We glided under low bridges and around narrow bends, as our personable student-guide simplified the architectural differences of the old houses. "There are three major shapes to the gables: neck, clock, and steps. The hooks at the top are used for hoisting furniture and other heavy loads up into buildings whose stairways are prohibitively narrow." Once through the network of canals, we toured the large harbour and ended at the oldest section of the city, the sailors' playground, or as our pert guide phrased it, "They come here for drinks, dancing and bad reputations."

Amsterdam is a very lively city with street youth playing flutes, strumming guitars and executing sidewalk paintings. Their legacy for tolerance dates from the 1600s when they started to trade with the rest of the world. The "bad reputations" sat on window ledges and reached out for David from the door jambs. I kept a firm hold on his arm. Our boat guide had told us that the city has one million inhabitants and one half million bicycles, many of them offered free for the day. It is easy to believe as you watch them whizzing past slower moving trams, buses and cars, a pretty girl with a wicker basket of bread and tulips on the front and a blond baby in a seat at the back. Whole families race down one of the specially built bike sidewalks, as people stand aside laughing and cheering them on.

Bad weather drove us the next day into a museum, but the *Rijksmuseum* was one that we would not have wanted to miss. The Dutch artists celebrated the ordinary things in life: a maid pouring a pitcher of milk, a domestic scene that suggested layers of meaning below its impeccable surface, a still life of fruits and flowers. These painters seemed to concentrate on capturing a kitchen moment. Here was the subject matter that would be the focus of our professional lives painted with compassion by Rembrandt, Vermeer and de Hooch. The lower floor of the museum was deserted, so I had the wonderful doll's house all to myself. It is historically accurate with painted ceilings, delft tiles and silverware on carpeted tables, as we had noticed in life size Dutch homes.

I hit the jackpot for children's playthings in a dusty mask-party games-tricks kind of shop. The disinterested owner barely had the energy to reach up to one of the shelves for a cardboard box when I asked if he had any scraps. Before he could fall asleep, I bought the entire box of antique embossed Austrian scraps made in the golden age of lithography. Next door, a used book store had a copy of William Morris' *News from Nowhere*, in which he describes a Utopian world, rural, peaceful and attractive. We drove into it the next day.

The best way to appreciate Amsterdam's unique architecture
is from a barge on the canal.

May 7, 1969   EDAM

Edam (it should have been Eden) is a quiet, pretty place paved in red brick with neat gardens fronting small, gabled houses, some of which serve as stores, with unobtrusive printed signs designating their business. Housewives and farmworkers wore the traditional wooden shoes. Narrow wooden lift bridges bring Van Gogh's painting to life. Our campsite was on the edge of the sea that borders the Netherlands. We carried our picnic meal up on to a narrow ridge of grass where sheep were resting to watch the reflections of the setting sun on the waves. Suddenly it dropped behind the dark silhouettes of the sheep, leaving a magenta-streaked sky.

Our meal that night, perched on the edge of a dyke that was holding back the North Sea, was as typical as the setting - smoked mackerel, *genever* (the local gin) and a chunk of Edam cheese. The liquor was new to us, as all of our drinking experiences on this trip had been. As young Presbyterians, living in Canada in our twenties, we had not seen, yet alone tasted, the array of spirits hidden behind the walls of the LCBO. These travels opened yet another closet.

It started with single malt tastings in the Highlands of Scotland. Whisky was not hidden; it was celebrated. The centuries-old distilleries toured us around their giant copper brewing kettles and malting barrels. A wee dram with a splash of water from a hillside stream kept the cold mists at bay. It was dribbled on salmon and oatmeal. My relatives opened a bottle and offered a glass with a gammon sandwich when we came to visit.

English pubs introduced us to the social side of imbibing. After trudging through villages in the rain, we gathered with the locals around coal fires in sixteenth century inns to quaff some strong cider, ale or even honey mead. Before the start of a Boxing Day Hunt, we sipped a glass of sherry with the red-coated riders. For 1968 Christmas dinner, I bought a half bottle of Bordeaux Graves 1962 from Fortnum and Masons, and David poured cognac on the pudding.

After observing two quite proper older ladies in a small Spanish restaurant consume a full bottle of red wine with a paella, we were convinced that it must be the accepted custom. We hung a straw-covered flask from the ceiling in the van and learned how to squirt wine directly into our mouths from a leather skin. Spanish brandy was a great comfort late at night in the van.

Our introduction to the classic wines of France and Italy was a social revelation. On our drive through lands planted with vines, we saw four generations seated under trees, eating local produce as they raised glasses of their own vintages. Italian youngsters added a drop or two of Chianti to their mineral water. Wine and food seemed inseparable; yet not once that year did we stumble upon a sorry drunk by the roadside. Moderation and enjoyment were the standards.

Now we were in Holland, a country associated with beer, sipping *genever*, the most popular liquor in the Netherlands. It has a long history, starting as a spirit that tasted more like whisky than the current gin-flavour, introduced by the inclusion of juniper berries. It was christened *Dutch Courage* by British troops fighting in Holland and has come to embody the spirit of the people. Our experiences of eating and drinking close to the land that year made us aware that the national brew was a proud part of the culture of a country.

Edam has wooden lift bridges, canals with bicycle tow paths,
flowering trees and great cheese.

May 8, 1969   HAMBURG

We needed to cross back into Germany to reach the ferry that would take us to Denmark. The tall Maypoles were still standing in this part of the country, entwined with cedar boughs, ribbons of every colour falling from the top. Young girls would have danced around this pole on the first of May, weaving the ribbons into a tight plait by ducking under and over each other's strand.

I was reading quietly by the van window at our campsite in Hamburg when David drew my attention to the blue van parked next to us. A bald man was feeding large hunks of raw, red meat to what looked at first like a large dog, but on closer inspection turned out to be a panther. Then I noticed its mate sitting just inside the van. I was relieved to see a leather halter on both of them. Unfortunately, it wasn't fastened to anything and the one on the grass managed to cover the few yards between us before his owner reigned him in. For the rest of our short stay here, we never left our van without first checking the back door of the blue van.

Hamburg was not all red meat. The source notes on the back of *La Belle Jardinere* series of prints I had purchased in Freiburg, indicated that the originals were hanging in *der Museum fur Kunst and Gewerbe* (Decorative Arts and Crafts) in Hamburg. A forty-five minute tram ride brought us to its doors. I not only enjoyed seeing my turn-of-the- century lady gardeners in poster size, there were also several rooms of early nineteen hundreds Morris-influenced furnishings and *Jugendstil* decorative objects.

The northern part of Germany was so free of traffic that we made it to the Puttgarden ferry in one day rather than two. We also misjudged the crossing time to the Danish island of Zealand, on which Cøpenhagen is located. David thought it was a three hour sail, and certainly the ample smorgasbord laid out in the dining room indicated a longish ride. We were well into our third helpings of smoked fish and meatballs when the announcement came through the speakers that we were approaching the landing dock at *Rodbyhavn*, three-quarters of an hour after departure. We had managed to stow away three hours worth of food.

DENMARK
Designed for Living

May 10, 1969   COPENHAGEN

The literal translation of *København*, the Danish spelling of the capital city, Copenhagen, is *merchants' harbour*. At the end of the journey, we had sailed into the right port. Denmark was also the perfect last stop of our trip because it combined a reputation for being gifted in design with a sense of fun. Andersen created magic from ordinary domestic objects - tin soldiers made from teaspoons, darning needles that have adventures, teapots, street lamps, flying trunks, tinder boxes, a child who sells matches, all took on a significance that transcended their simplicity. Our discoveries in Copenhagen were coloured by a sense of light-hearted adventure, partly due to the nature of this city, but mostly due to Roger and Phyllis.

They were our neighbours in the *Gladsaxe* campsite, an excellent facility that had been recommended to us months earlier by a fellow-camper in Italy. Roger had been an ambulance driver for the American army in Europe. He and Phyllis were married by the captain of a sailboat somewhere in the Mediterranean. Their tales of the camel market in Morocco, the Wall in Berlin and the jaunt through Yugoslavia to Greece, made us feel like milque-toasts. After a quick exchange of pleasantries, he said "It's a great day for you guys to take in Tivoli Gardens. Gives you the handle on this town. Tomorrow the four of us could catch some free beers on the Tuborg Brewery Tour." Sounded like a good plan.

Because these pleasure gardens are located right beside the City Hall

Strøget was the first and longest pedestrianized street in Europe.

in the centre of the city, they are accessible to anyone at any time with opening hours stretching from ten a.m. to midnight. This is no suburban theme park surrounded by acres of barren parking. Since 1895 these gardens have been a showcase of Danish design, as well as a place to have a great time. Take the tea pavilion, for instance, predictably our first stop when we arrived. A table with a proper cloth was set on a terrace near the small lake, bordered with a sampling of the half a million flowers blooming at any time in these gardens. We were served tea and a selection of this country's famous pastries on Royal Copenhagen porcelain. A subsequent forty years of being served tea in styrofoam cups made me doubt the accuracy of this recollection, so I called a Danish neighbour for confirmation. "Oh yes", replied Ulla, "As a matter of fact, the Royal Copenhagen Company had a small pavilion where you could have the satisfaction of smashing their flawed pieces of dinnerware. The men used to take out any marital frustrations by throwing the national crockery against the walls in Tivoli."

In the centre of a pond, instead of the classical stone god or goddess fountain, a blue and white porcelain maiden with an upturned pointed nose, spouted water from her arms. A troop of red and blue uniformed soldiers, the Tivoli Boy Guard Marching Band, proudly strut the grounds, young boys who might have marched out of the musical stage production of *The Chocolate Soldier* before parading here. We observed all this from a bench beside several seniors who were obviously regular visitors to the gardens. "If you are a pensioner, you receive a special pass that allows you to come in and enjoy an afternoon just listening to the music and eating an ice cream as I am doing now. But as a visitor, you really must come back tonight when Tivoli shimmers." It was heartening to know that the Danes offered flexible prices and hours of operation so that young and old alike could enjoy this popular amusement park, whose focus was not solely on the bottom line.

We did return to the gardens that night and the old gentleman was correct - they are transformed. Thousands of lights outline the roofs, domes and turrets of the theatres, pavilions and bandshells, casting their reflections into the lake that once was the moat around the town fortifications. Admission was free to the bright, airy concert hall, whose glass walls allowed you to watch the merry-go-round outside while enjoying the light operas of Strauss, Lehar and Offenbach inside. The musicians teased us by singing the first few bars of the more popular melodies, just to get us smiling. Occasionally, a scream from the roller coaster added a high note to the music.

The open-air stage across from the concert hall featured Tania, the dancing elephant, with a team of acrobats. On the other side of the lake, a Rock and Roll Dance Pavilion was pumping out the heavier beat of a live group. Pierrot and Columbine provide an historical link with the traditional *Commedia del Arte* every evening. But their ballet is an informal slapstick interpretation of the original. For me, the star of the show was the oriental scarlet and gold Peacock Pantomime Theatre, whose stage curtain is the bird's open fan tail. Tubs of white lilacs, in full fragrant bloom, lined the entrance path to the theatre. As we stood on the bridge looking down at the thousands of lights on the water (no neon allowed) a blaze of fireworks lit the City Hall's red brick tower. Something for every taste here, in more than one sense. Over thirty restaurants, including some of Denmark's finest chefs, serve a wide variety of meals on the grounds to meet every price range.

If you were to take a reading of the national pulse here, you would find that it is a strong, hearty beat. Unlike other nations' attempts at amusement parks, Tivoli successfully combines innocent fun with elegance; childish delight with an appreciation of civilized niceties.

Roger and Phyllis were the ideal companions for this city - adventurous, light-hearted, entertaining. No other city would have put up with their shenanigans without wagging the finger. The four of us decided to stroll *Strøget*, Europe's first and longest pedestrian shoppers' street which cuts right through the heart of the old city. On one of the pleasant open market squares, Roger picked up a purple egg carton, wove two pieces of found ribbon through the corners, and tied it onto Phyllis' head. She smiled under her new bonnet, posed for a photo and continued the walk as though he had just bought her a present from one of the fine boutiques. While Phyllis and I went into Illum's Department store to check out the latest in housewares, Roger assumed the yogic position near a wheelbarrow full of fresh daffodils. The broad-minded Danes are generous in their acceptance of eccentrics and barely blinked as they walked around him. The four of us lined up at a pølse wagon to try these wieners without buns. You dip the long thin sausage into a bit of mustard and eat it without a wrap. We became pølse addicts and would line up every time we saw a wagon. Once Roger had us lined up beside a tar wagon before the smell gave away his game.

The four of us sat nibbling shrimp open-face sandwiches (which I christened, Danwiches) on the edge of a fountain, enjoying a passing military band and a troupe of clowns from the Schumann circus. We lost Roger for a few minutes while he joined the clowns, but he returned eager to start a discussion on touristic photographic techniques. David confessed that he usually studied a rack of postcards and tried to line up similar camera angles. Roger suggested that we continue down *Strøget* to the sailors' quarter at *Nyhavn* to test this approach. In this colourful harbour area you can hear the buzz of the tattoo needle and choose a design from the window display. That's not the only diversion sitting in these windows. Roger focused his camera on a couple of the local call girls as he commented, "You won't find this shot on any postcards."

I had to return to Strøget on my own the next day to pay some serious homage at the Royal Copenhagen showrooms. Ever since my teenage summer job in a china store, I have had an appreciation of fine dinnerware and *Flora Danica* is the best I've seen. Painted bouquets of Scandinavian flora twine around cream jug and gravy boat handles that are shaped like twigs. In the centre of each elaborately gilt-edged plate is a scientifically accurate botanical study of a plant found in Denmark. When New York's Cooper-Hewitt Museum mounted an exhibit of antique pieces in this line, the curator, David McFadden noted, "The *Flora Danica* porcelain was a very important example in the late eighteenth century of bringing the worlds of science and art together." I would expand his point to include commerce, for this product still has buyers, even at the high prices required to justify its manufacture. From its conception it has connected many disciplines - compiled by a scientist, engraved by an artist, painted by a craftsman, manufactured for royalty and now for sale to the public. On the back of each piece, the painter writes his initials beside the three wavy blue lines, the Royal Copenhagen hallmark representing the three bodies of water that flow around Denmark.

A display of silver jewellery in one of the spiffier store windows caught my attention. The stylized hammered tulip brooch could have come from one of the pages in a 1920s book, *Designing from Plant Forms*, we had purchased on our travels. A biography inside the store explained that the silversmith, Georg Jensen, had been inspired by two of his near contemporaries - William Morris' concept of the artist-craftsman and Charles Rennie Mackintosh's art nouveau lines. The naturalistic motifs, a swirl of sterling studded with an oval green agate, marked a fresh approach to Celtic design. The marriage of the Danish Princess Alexandra to Queen Victoria's eldest son, Edward, helped to lubricate this flow of ideas between nations. Jensen was our Danish link to the Arts and Crafts movement we had been following across Europe. The Danes had their own term for this style, *Skønvirke*, which means, "beautiful work".

Georg Jensen was able to develop his artistry in a more far-reaching practical way than his predecessors. His wide range of domestic holloware including wine goblets, serving dishes, gravy boats, pitchers, barware, tea sets and tureens, brought his country into the international spotlight. Jensen stores opened on the main avenues of New York and Paris, selling flatware to grace the tables of discerning hostesses. Just a few years before my visit to this flagship store in Copenhagen, the Wor-

Entrance to the harbour district of Copenhagen.

David at the Tea Pavilion in Tivoli Gardens with the
City Hall in the background.

shipful Company of Goldsmiths in London had honoured the art of Georg Jensen with a centenary exhibition at Goldsmiths Hall.

The city had already won me over with its sense of proportion and functional aesthetics, but when I realized that it was a bicycle haven I almost dropped anchor. The Danes were quick to realize that people could relax, stroll, talk and shop much more comfortably if they did not have to fight the noise and fumes of the automobile. Consequently, the bicycle is the Copenhageners preferred means of transit. Any morning we went into town, we'd be passed by a stream of bikes with everything from briefcases to bedrolls strapped onto their racks. Families take biking holidays on the miles of paths provided and tourists can rent or even borrow two wheels from train stations or municipal bike racks. They are committed environmentalists who take pleasure in being as close to the natural beauty of their countryside as possible. It's another example of their ability to have innocent fun in attractive surroundings. We felt that Copenhagen was the ideal end to this part of our journey. Months of new experiences over thousands of miles of road had left us in awe of the French, Germans, Spanish and Italians, but it was the Danish poetic realism I ended up admiring the most. They had met the challenge of devising an export trade with limited raw materials in a small country, by wisely nurturing their craftsmen. They have gained world-wide recogniton as leaders in the design and manufacture of beautiful and functional objects for everyday life and invest heavily in cultural activities.

OPEN-FACE SANDWICHES

Our Danish neighbour, Ulla, prefers I use this title, rather than Danwiches, which is simply not in the Danish lexicon. An international sandwich spread is the perfect way to close our culinary odyssey as you can include breads, meats and cheeses from all the countries we passed through. You can set all the ingredients out on large platters to let guests make their own combo-sandwich or prepare your time-tested combinations. Ulla's favourite is the creamed shrimp on white bread; ours is smoked salmon spread on light rye. Men head for roast beef with Asiago.

Adjust quantities to your needs.

SHRIMP DANWICH

INGREDIENTS
1/2 cup of tiny frozen shrimp, peeled, deveined, cut in half
1/4 cup mayonnaise
1-1/2 tablespoons chopped fresh basil leaves
1 teaspoon lemon juice
pinch of salt and pepper
rectangles of buttered bread
twists of lemon for garnish

METHOD
1. Mix the mayo, basil, and seasonings together.
2. Toss in the prepared shrimp to coat.
3. Mound onto the buttered bread.
4. Cut a thin half slice of lemon down the centre so that you can twist it to set on top.

CREAMED SMOKED SALMON ON CUCUMBERS

INGREDIENTS

This amount will make dozens of two inch open-face rounds. I keep what is not used immediately in a covered crock in the fridge for up to a week.

4 ounces of smoked salmon cut into small pieces

2 ounces unsalted butter

2 tablespoons sour cream

pinch of cayenne pepper

a few grinds of whole white pepper

1 teaspoon lemon juice

enough thinly sliced cucumber for the amount of sandwiches being made

a loaf of light rye bread

fresh dill for garnish

METHOD

1. Use the on/off motion of a food processor to finely mince the salmon.
2. Incorporate the butter in pieces.
3. Whirl in the remaining ingredients one at a time, stopping to scrape down the sides frequently.
4. Use a two inch circular biscuit cutter to cut rounds from the bread. Place a cucumber slice on each.
5. Spread a teaspoonful of salmon on each cucumber.
6. Top with a small frond of dill.

BEEF WITH SLICED ASIAGO

INGREDIENTS

thin slices of peppered roasted beef (your own or from the deli counter)

2 tablespoons sour cream

1/2 cup horseradish

dark rye bread or pumpernickel

thin slices of Asiago or Havarti cheese (according to preference)

cornichon pickles

METHOD

1. Stir sour cream into horseradish.
2. Cut the slices of bread into halves.
3. Spread liberally with the creamed horseradish.
4. Lay on several thin slices of beef.
5. Cover with one slice of cheese.
6. Top with a small pickle cut into a fan shape.

GERMANY

May 19, 1969 HAMBURG

We enjoyed our last pølse while waiting for the ferry to arrive from *Puttgarden* to carry us back to Germany. We returned to the Hamburg campsite for the night. The big cats were still there.

May 20 - 22, 1969 BREMEN

The van was to be shipped back to Canada from *Bremer-haven*. Empty. Several hurdles had to be jumped in two days - buy a trunk or trunks to pack everything that was currently in the van. Get these trunks sent off from a train station where tickets could be purchased for our return to Britain. Deliver the empty van to the port and wave it goodbye. But this city is no mere industrial complex and cannot simply be written off as "a place to ship the van from." Rather than packing, we took the first day to tour the city.

We immediately noticed that it had been able to retain the charm of its past while filling its role as Germany's second largest port. The original ramparts are now a green girdle skirting the centre of the city with an old mill and parkland following the course of what appears to be a moat. So you can have "a walk along the wall" so to speak, with ducks and rhododendrons on either side. The market square is crammed with interesting statuary and architecture. A huge stone statue

In a Grimms Brothers' fairy tale, a donkey, a dog, a cat and a rooster run away from their farmyard to become musicians.

The giant Roland is the Frankish hero of the legendary *Chanson de Roland* and the protector of the city of Bremen.

of the giant, Roland, protector of the city, was erected in 1404. He is a hero in the *Chanson de Roland*, a Frankish military leader under Charlmagne who stands proudly in front of the Gothic *Rathaus*. This ornate Town Hall boasts a *Ratskeller* storing gigantic wine barrels and hundreds of German wines, including the twelve oldest wines in the world.

To the right rise the twin pencils of St. Peter's Cathedral and across the way stands the golden Merchant's Guild. The statue of a rooster standing on a cat, who is standing on a dog, who in turn is on a donkey, testify that this is the home of the Brother Grimms' fairy tale *The Bremen Town Musicians*. According to the story, these four animals were considered past their prime by the farmer, who was planning to get rid of them. They decided to run away to the town of Bremen where they would be free to become musicians. The donkey's front hooves are shiny from people rubbing them to make their wishes come true.

This last market square of the trip was a winner.

Just off the square, a golden St. Michael flies across a brick archway to indicate the entrance to the *Bottcherstrasse*, an medieval craftsmen's alley, whose buildings were daringly converted in the 1920s to a Gothic/Art Nouveau street of museums and shops where artisans make and sell glass, pottery, pewter, wood and leather objects. The narrow, eclectic red brick street is punctuated by quiet courtyards with fountains and statuary.

The *Schnoor Quarter* near the *Neser River* is the oldest remaining residential area of Bremen, with houses dating from the 16th to the 18th centuries. At street level, these historic buildings become pubs, galleries, restaurants and antique shops. In one of these, an eccentric old chap ran the German counterpart of a Victoriana store with toy soldiers, old post cards and posters. Even though it was our last afternoon and we still had not packed, we added to our pile by buying some old lithographs and three Prussian toy soldiers.

Somehow, the chores got done without problems. The purchase of two tin trunks, the feat of packing clothing, camping equipment, books and enough stock to open a store, was all accomplished smoothly and before we knew it, the empty van was on its way to Canada and we were seated on the 5:15 Scandinavian Express clipping along to *Hook van Holland*, where a boat was waiting to carry us across to Harwich and the English countryside. Even seen through the train window, the gentle green fields had us rummaging through our hand baggage for the poetry books.

The van had to be emptied and sent off from the Bremen harbour,
yet Ann continues to gaze in shop windows along an old craftsmen's street.

ENGLAND

May 23, 1969, LONDON

Business before pleasure. At the Canadian Pacific offices on Trafalgar Square, we straightened out some minor snags by booking a sailing a week earlier from Greenock, enabling us to arrive in Montreal not much later than the van. The C.P. kindly arranged to send their vans around to collect our myriad trunks which had been left with Aunt Esther in Glasgow.

Next stop was the Canadian branch of our bank on Berkeley Square where we withdrew our $500 balance then headed straight to Leicester Square to spend a chunk of it on theatre tickets. This last week in London, we were to see *She Stoops to Conquer*, starring Tom Courtney; *Isadora*, to put us in the correct Zen frame of mind; and *Anne of Green Gables*, because we'd have to re-enter that culture soon.

Over to Hatchard's on Piccadilly Street where we bought *Fantastic Costumes of Trades and Professions*, a portfolio of engravings that were to provide the blueprints for the first signage to hang above our store.

May 24, 1969

David generously gave me a small kitty from the remaining money to stock up on some Victoriana. I blew it all the next day out at Blackheath Market. Down a small alley was a wonderful bookstore that had complete Victorian scrap books filled with original collections. I did not hesitate. Next door took care of any remaining money - beaded bags, silver tea spoons and an 1860 bound edition of the *London Illustrated*

News. I just had time to stuff them into the trunk before the lorry drove it to the docks.

May 28, 1969

So much for the Victoriana. Now for the kitchenwares. I telephoned Elizabeth David's Kitchen Shop and got the owner herself. I told her of our plans and she was supportive, even giving me the name of a British exporter of tin bakeware, Tala, and another fine old firm, Rushbrooke's, who sold the traditional striped butchers' aprons and some French woodware. I took the tube around to her store to say a personal thanks, pick up the latest catalogue and buy one of the round wire egg baskets that had hung in her window on our first visit and that I hadn't been able to find in France.

May 29, 1969

The Flying Scotsman was the name of the train that took us back up to Glasgow. Aunt Esther was still sitting by the fire. "Well, did ye have a grand time o'er the water?"

"Words canna say."

CANADA
June - July, 1969 AGAWA BAY

The decision to hide up on the north shore of Lake Superior for the rest of the summer was made when we were about ten miles out of Montreal. It had been two harrowing days since we left the sanctuary of the *Empress of England*, severing all ties with the world of elevenses on deck, free movies, regular full-course meals and McAndrews and Mills in the cabaret. Now everything seemed foreign in our homeland, as though we were passing through another country. But this stop would be a long one in a world of cars, stores, highways and garages that seemed bigger than they needed to be. The only cause for celebration so far was reclaiming our beagle Tippy in Windsor. Those five children had not walked the dog as promised, so the parents had banished her to Tobacco Road on the outskirts of the city, where we found her chained to a rusted truck, covered with grease and jubilant at the sight of us. We dognapped her, tossed her into the van and now all three of us howl at the moon every night on a northern shore.

Agawa Bay restored our equilibrium. We set up camp at the end of Rocky Point, cooked over a wood fire on the beach - eggs, bacon, burgers and beans mainly- Wawa's selection was limited. But running along the beach with Tippy every morning and sitting beside a fire under a canopy of stars every night, almost made it seem all right. Weekends were the worst. Campers came to let off steam and have a good time, which included tossing firecrackers into the steel garbage pails, heaving rocks at the chipmunks and diving drunk off Rocky Point.

In the mid-week calm David got out his oil paints and I found that native wildflowers were a real pleasure to watercolour. On the night of July 20, so clear that we could see the craters on the moon, we sat looking out of the van windshield while the radio broadcast Neil Armstrong's historic sentence, "*One small step for man, one large step for mankind.*" It was time for us to make our move. We buried a time capsule with our hopes for the future in a tin can under a northern pine. Then we drove down to London, Ontario to start making them happen with the few hundred dollars we had left.

THE TEMPERATURE AT
WHICH BOOKS BURN
451 Dundas Street,
August 1969 LONDON ONTARIO

From our campsite at Fanshawe Park, David drove to the University of Western Ontario campus to register for post-graduate courses and collect a small stipend for signing up as a teaching assistant. I registered for classes in William Morris. It seemed appropriate to study a retailer/domestic/poet at this point. In the mornings over the campfire, I scoured the FOR RENT columns of *The London Free Press*, trying to find store premises with living quarters above. We had not a single friend, family member, or casual acquaintance in this city to offer advice on potentially promising locations. Gut instinct proved superior to anything the real estate agents had shown us. After several wasted afternoons looking at dud listings on main throughways on the edge of suburbia, I went back to the personal columns. A promising ad offered a store front with two large display windows on the main street, kitchen at the rear, bed, bath, living room upstairs. I took a dime to the phone booth and secured our first premises. It would be like going back to the Glasgow tenement set-up of my childhood, living above the store.

London, Ontario held a treasury of yellow brick Victorian architecture, commercial as well as residential, and with luck on our side, we had become tenants of one. But it was a grand dame down on her luck. Worn woodwork sagged around the three upper windows with broken panes. The bricks on the lower half had been covered by a board painted neon blue. Signage ran across the entire front proclaiming it to be the home of K&N Musical Instruments. With a street number 451, the temperature at which books burn, it was not an auspicious home for our collection of rare volumes. Altogether a daunting project for two untested entrepreneurs with no capital or experience. But the accommodating landlord agreed to a low rent in lieu of minimal repairs and our labour. We set about transporting traditional business practices, gathered from market places and narrow shopping streets on to Dundas Street, London, Ontario.

Standing in front of this unpromising premise, I closed my eyes and thought of England - of Regency shop fronts, muted tones of slate, touches of polished brass and imaginative trade signs. After absorbing merchandising concepts like a pair of solar panels for almost a year, we were keen to put pent-up creative energy to work. Every aspect of our formulative trip, museum exhibits, book/antique/kitchenwares stores, auction rooms, architecture, markets, art exhibits and country homes was incorporated in some way into that fledgling store. David drove the van out to scrap yards and returned with storm windows and carved walnut spindles to replace the gaps in our banister. We were pleased to have an original turned-spindle stairway, even if a few were missing. The landlord suggested blocking it in with plywood, but David scoured the wreckers' yards until he found a decent spindle match. It was all about bringing something back to its glory days, capturing a concrete part of lost time. On a broader scale, once you bring one building back from the brink, the whole neighbourhood turns around in a domino effect. Within a year of our opening, small restaurants and art stores were moving onto the block. A coat of soft grey paint transformed the bottom half of the store front. We lacquered the door black and added a brass letter slot and handle. It was our intention to make Ann McColl's look solid and professional, classic rather than cute. At a second-hand shop we found two coal scuttles. Filled with scarlet geraniums, they greeted customers with a Hestian welcome.

The location offered some pleasant bonuses. One block east, stands a large turreted Romanesque Revival building, originally called Oakhurst in 1887. Records in the local archives room of our library explain that the members of the Canadian Legion had formed a

Tweedsmuir Branch in 1936 with the approval of the first Baron Tweedsmuir (John Buchan), who immediately became the Honourable President of this branch of the legion, which he visited three times while he held the office of Governor General of Canada. His coat-of-arms was emblazoned on their cap badge. In 1945 the legion purchased Oakhurst, renamed it Buchan House and set up a limited company to take care of its daily operation. His son assumed the office after John died and kept in contact with this branch of the legion. It became a private men's club for a few years, until it came up for auction and was purchased by a lady who operated a home for blues music. When asked why she invested in this particular building, she replied, "Character. It's got Character." As did John Buchan, founder of our Governor General Awards for literature.

Anderson's Art Store, three doors down, anchored the corner. Brian Jones, one of London's young artists, lived above this meeting place for many of the city's other bright young painters. Across from it sat the Art Annex of Beal Vocational School, where London's finest teachers, nationally recognized artists, held day jobs. Each day, as we scrubbed, painted, swept and polished, they stopped by one by one to encourage us in our efforts at neighbourhood improvement and to welcome us to a group of people who cared. Gill Moll, one of the artists who stopped to chat, looked very much like the young William Morris. As a draughtsman and a print maker, he also shared the same interests. He agreed to illustrate our store sign using two copies of engravings from *Fantastic Costumes of Trades and Professions*, a portfolio of prints we had brought back from England. We commissioned him to paint large reproductions of two itinerant tradesmen, to flank each side of the store name. In the eighteenth century, there were many vendors who walked the streets with trays slung around their necks and merchandise dangling from every part of their body. One that we chose was an ironmonger, with a cauldron for a hat, roasting spits slung over his shoulder, a grid iron dangling from his fingers. He was girdled with saucepans, salvers, sieves and shovels. The companion sign showed a hooper, a craftsman who worked with thin circles of wood to fashion small household articles. His chest was an open cabinet revealing graduated sizes of wooden storage boxes. Stools, drum sieves and scoops hung from his waist. An elegant bamboo mesh covered tray was suspended from his hand. In between these figures, the store name, *Ann McColl's Kitchen Utensils and Victoriana*, paid homage to grandma Annie McColl and stamped our business with the same personal commitment shown by Elizabeth David's, a unique statement on the front of a small shop in 1960s Ontario. Our intention from the first was to make a visible alliance between the arts and commerce, a small stab at nurturing a cultural economy.

The interior presented more of a challenge. The path to the furnace at the rear of the basement was blocked by hundreds of empty rye bottles and defunct pinball machines that all had to be hand removed. Within the first month we found out who had emptied the bottles. One night, while David was stretched out on the couch downstairs, watching television with Tippy dozing on his lap, two vagrants tried to climb in through my bedroom window (while I was in the bed). Neither the guard dog or the man of the house stirred. When the police arrived, they told me that the guys thought it was still their home. The location definitely needed an image over-haul.

The first thing David did was build enough upstairs shelving to hold most of our stock, so that he wouldn't keep cracking his skull on the low beams in that basement. With visions of the Habitat store dancing in my head, we painted the front room white and laid down a sisal mat floor covering. David bought a Victorian pine fireplace surround with an ornate black cast iron oval screen from a psychiatric hospital due for demolition. Hammered into the wall under a defunct stove pipe, it became the feature for a display of cast iron and copper kettles, cauldrons and skillets. We suspended Uncle Joe's iron griddle from its grate. Shiny tin eclair pans, madeleine moulds, fluted brioche forms, lidded pudding steamers, springform cake tins and ice cream bombes (as illustrated in my copy of *Mrs. Beeton's*) sparkled on the open shelves of an old hutch top which had been painted electric blue. An antique pastry-rolling table held a selection of crimped cutters, shortbread presses and crocks of wooden spoons. A large rectangle of marble, formerly a dividing wall in the girls' washroom of the public school where I had taught, was set onto a cast iron base to hold cream-coloured mixing bowls filled with French whisks. I remember our landlord, curious at this transformation of his property, picking up one of these whisks, waving it in circles over his head as he asked, "You're going to pay the rent selling these?" I positioned myself firmly behind the oak teacher's desk, also salvaged from the first school where I had taught and stated, "You'll get it every month on the dot." One month after we had watched Neil Armstrong take his first step on the moon, we were ready to open the door on our first step into the business world.

Three months after our return to Canada, *Ann McColl's Kitchen Utensils and Victoriana* opened at 451 Dundas Street.

August 26, 1969 OPENING DAY

A lithograph, purchased that last afternoon in Bremen, a Victorian scrap of two chubby Austrian children clutching tulips, announced times of opening on the front door. A brass bell rang every time a customer came through the door. They passed under a framed lithograph of Queen Victoria dressed for her Diamond Jubilee celebrations. Odd to think, that in the year of the publication of this book, her great-great-grand-daughter, Elizabeth II will be celebrating her Diamond Jubilee, sixty years on the throne.

Every sale was recorded on a carbon copy hand-written receipt. At the end of the first day, I was thrilled to total the collection on my steel spike — twenty-five dollars! I read it as an augury of instant success. At the turn of the millennium, a loyal first customer sent me a copy of her receipt, kept since 1969. It listed:

> *garlic press - $1.95*
> *grater - .35*
> *John Ruskin - $1.25*
> *Poetry of Flowers - $3.50*
> *Virgil's Aeneid - .50*

She kindly noted on her card that she considered the opening of the kitchen shop one of the main events of the last century. The books on her list came from the tall mahogany secretaire, purchased at auction and set up in the small room dedicated to books and prints, behind the front sales room. The fact that our premise had the number 451 over the door did not seem to hamper our book sales. Soon our collection of antiquarian leather-bounds, gathered on the tour around England was scooped up, so David started buying boxfulls at auction. We made one astute buyer very happy when we sold him a first edition Susanna Moodie, *Roughing it in the Bush*, for very little. We had a lot to learn about this trade.

Our artist neighbours supported us with praise and purchases. Larry Russell commented on the purity of our roll of kraft wrapping paper mounted on the wall, "like a still-life" he said. Greg and Sheila Curnoe bought white jugs for their *café au lait*. Paterson Ewen picked up the magic lantern and slides we had brought back from an English flea market. Ron Martin bought a round pedestal oak table for the centre of his studio. Tom and Ron Benner made a pine cupboard. Terry was a gifted local interior designer and socialite. Late at night, he would say to company, "I'm feeling blue. Let's go down to look in Ann McColl's window." Maybe Tedward, our resident teddy bear, sitting on a checkered picnic cloth with a pot of *hunny* in front of him, would cheer him up.

One of the locals fell in love with this bear, but he was a special find, not for sale. Every morning I would bicycle to the charity shops to scour their kitchen utensil bins for collectible pieces of enamelware or interesting tin moulds. One day I spotted this personable old bear languishing in the Salvation Army used toy bin. I ransomed him with a dollar bill, christened him Tedward, plunked him into the bicycle basket and pedaled him home to preside over the children's book section in our back room. Tedward soon became a goodwill ambassador for the business, but he would let out a low growl if you squeezed his tummy. We stocked copies of *The Pooh Cookbook*, published by McClelland & Stewart Ltd., 1969, the year we opened the shop.

When Tedward put on his striped butcher's apron we moved him into the kitchenware section. It was only natural that trade in honey pots and twirling sticks would soar under his watch. At an antique store in the country we bought a Victorian pressback highchair for Ted. Children's dinnerware sales were given a boost when his tray was set with plates and mugs that depicted bears. In the summer, he held court on a red checked tablecloth spread out in the front window with a picnic basket and accessories.

It was in this role that he caught the eye of a local artist who asked permission to take him to her studio to pose for a series of drawings. When his stay in bohemia became extended, I called for his return to work. A cab pulled up in front of the shop and a slightly bemused driver came in to announce, "I've got a bear on the back seat for you, lady." Tedward was clutching some First Edition Canadian Artist Series bookplates which depicted him sitting in apron and chef's hat with a cookbook open on his lap and a note on the back urging borrowers to return their friends' books with something warm from the oven.

We must have established a reputation for this kind of merchandising, because one day a young career woman with a briefcase came into the store and announced, "I'm the Pooh co-ordinator for Eatons department store. Could you give me some tips?" I pointed to our smug-looking bear and said, "Ask him."

These promotional quirks in this strange little shop appealed to the media. *The London Free Press* printed a photograph of Tippy the beagle in a nineteenth century pram to announce the opening of that first kitchen-antiques shop. Our aged hound stares out at the public, squeezed in front of rolls of wrapping paper, looking very concerned in the Victorian baby buggy. And rightly so. She gave birth to a litter shortly after. Only one lively, black-haired pup, whom we christened Winston, survived, and he was quickly adopted by a customer.

She did not seem to mind being a career dog as opposed to a mother and quickly took control of the store floor. Tippy was sensitive to bad vibes, and did not believe that "the customer is always right." She would wriggle up to her favourites, white-tipped tail wagging, while others triggered the full beagle howl as soon as they crossed the threshold. It became necessary to confine her to the flat above the store where she stayed quiet until the magic hour of five o'clock. Then the head would get thrown back, the jowls rounded into an 0, and the whole building re-sounded as though the hounds from hell were above the store.

"What on earth is that?" amazed customers would ask.

"Just Tippy letting us know that it's half an hour until closing time."

She did appreciate the patch of grass we had salvaged of the yard be-hind the store. And so did David. He set up a tarp shelter for his furni-ture refinishing, bought belt sanders, planes, steel wool, tins of laquer stripper and finishing polish. Every Saturday he drove the van out into the country to bid against other dealers on cherry banc lits, pine hutches, walnut desks, harvest tables, maple corner cupboards and oak com-modes. He had a good eye for fine pieces of Canadiana and a knack for bringing out the beauty of the wood. It is no exaggeration to say that this aspect of the business did more for our bank balance than my care-fully selected *batterie de cuisine*. We still meet customers at the market who remind us that their family will eat tonight from the harvest table David refinished forty years ago, or that they store firewood in a pine box painted with oxblood, purchased from our store that first year.

Our primitive kitchen, down a small hallway behind the showroom, had wood dadoing and an open door policy. Customers could watch me rolling pie pastry, learning how to use the tools of my new trade, on a napkin-size counter. In one corner sat a gas stove that had survived the depression. I loved cooking on it. Compared to the camping gaz stove it was a true luxury, and filled the store with the aroma of onion soup or lamb stew. This nine by twelve foot room could not be used for proper demonstrations, but it could be used to measure the capacity of moulds, run a test on a teapot to see if the spout dripped, and develop recipe fliers to hand out. The local paper ran an illustrated article of a chicken roasted on a bed of vegetables in one of the "new" clay bakers in the back room kitchen cooker. We poured endless pots of tea that first year as we became acquainted with new sales reps and made friends out of customers. The silver cake stand, found at the rummage sale in the crypt of St-Martin-in-the-Fields, held slices of fruit flan and shortbread fingers. We sent customers home with printed recipes of *Grandma Grant's Shortbread* and *Bake a Flan in a Pan from Ann.*

Unorthodox retailing brings the press out in swarms. *The Gazette*, student newspaper for The University of Western Ontario, did a multi-page photo spread featuring our small sitting room which we had papered with a Morris design, the table set for high tea, with the suggestion that we might set up a Tea Room in the back. This association with food preparation on a personal level helped to establish our reputation as a shop for cooks right from the start. In over thirty years of business, we never had need for an advertising budget.

I learned a great deal from our customers, especially the one who was looking for a big soup pot to prepare Julia Child's bean soup with pesto. "Julia who?" I asked. She showed me her stained copy of *Mastering the Art of French Cooking*, and urged me to stock it on our shelves. Julia's ground-breaking *French Chef* programme out of Boston's Public Broadcasting Station, had started in the early sixties, when our heads were buried in term papers. By the end of the decade this unpretentious American was demystifying French cooking on over ninety PBS stations across America. Home cooks felt that if this large, slightly clumsy woman could do Beef Wellington, then they could too. All they needed was her excellent cookbook and the proper equipment. Julia had insisted on a straight sided soufflé dish to make this egg dessert rise properly and flan rings to bake quiche. She had been priming our customer base. By the time we opened, home chefs were walking through our door with a utensil shopping list. We couldn't have timed it better.

Another unforgettable customer was the serviceman who wanted to replace his Mouli grater. I was caught out again. He patiently explained that he had bought the first one while stationed at an airforce base in France decades ago and couldn't grate cheese or chocolate without it. I found a Montreal distributor and from then on was never without one, either in the store or in my own kitchen. This rotating drum grater turns a hard boiled egg into mimosa and a hunk of parmesan into snow with no skin off your knuckles. A salute to the overseas servicemen who bring home other cultures.

My favourite couple in over thirty years of retailing, walked into that first store one half hour before closing time on a snowy Christmas Eve. They were a charmed pair, full of a love for life and each other. I had just survived two months of serving the usual harried holiday shopper, uncertain, rushed, stressed by obligations. Now here were two spirited, inspired creatures who waltzed around our depleted displays at zero hour exclaiming, "Perfect skillet for Joe! Won't Alice adore this print?" No special wrapping requests. No "may-we-return-these" conditions. Before Tippy let out her closing howl, they gathered up their entire Christmas present list and glided out into the snow arm in arm. I never saw them again but will always remember them.

Forty years later I met one of our original customers at a seniors' exercise class. Susan had grown up in Germany. She squeezed my hand as she explained how over the years she brought her children to our store telling them that it was just like the small stores in Europe. She bought her spaetzle maker from us that first year and still uses it to press the dumpling dough over pots of stew. There were reasons why our store transported her to a different time and place. Stock did not arrive in containers; everything was independently sourced and bought because it was beautiful as well as useful. It was local and handcrafted or recycled when we could find it. Canadian wooden bowls, cutting boards and peppermills held pride of place. Hand carved English bread boards, Scottish shortbread presses engraved with thistles, rich earthen bowls thrown by gifted Canadian potters, sat on antique pine cupboards. All of the small tools and cooking equipment were relieved of their packaging before being piled in Indian baskets. We steered away from anything labelled *gimmick, gadget or gourmet*. Bouquets of fresh flowers and pots of herbs greeted our customers.

Ginette (Gina) Bisaillon was a very special customer right from her first visit, June 1972. She introduced herself with the announcement that she and her business partner, Robin Askew, would be opening an authentic French-Canadian restaurant right behind us, called *L'Auberge du Petit Prince*, and she would rely on us for certain items, but not much, as most equipment would be shipped from her Montreal home or overseas. If anyone could transform the red brick Ontario house into an *auberge*, it was this confident woman with her childhood love of author Antoine de Saint-Exupéry's little prince who cooked over volcanic jets on a far planet. Artist Bernice Vincent designed the logo used on business cards and the outdoor sign. In one seven-table dining room, Gina installed a handsome pine-mantled fireplace. We became immediate friends and I still marvel at the level of professionalism with which Ginette and Robin dazzled the city's élite. Gina was the talented chef who introduced Londoners to genuine French and Quebecois specialities. The menu changed daily, offering a choice from two or three appetizers and two or three entrées. Artist, Jamelie Hassan, was their reliable helper/server. Robin filled their cellar with fine wines and was such an exacting *maître d'hôtel* that forty years later David and I still find ourselves comparing her impeccable service with less competent wine stewards.

The kitchen was open to friends and all of London's artists on Twelfth Night, when Gina prepared an enormous cassoulet on the restaurant range and ladled beans in goose stock laced with tomatoes, garlic, and sausage onto our plates. For a few blessed years we shared a village on our block, a magic kingdom ruled by a little prince, descended from his gas-jet satellite.

David and I had both enrolled in The University of Western Ontario's graduate English courses, but before the first year was out, we knew that the business was going to demand all of our time. Besides, it was more fun than any classroom. Even on minimal earnings, we scraped enough together to each fly to England on separate inspirational buying trips. We called these refresher courses. David would buy a trunk, like the blue metal one that had accompanied us in the van, and drive around in a rented Morris Mini, picking up the list of old kitchen wares I had sent him off to find - fish knives and forks, glass jelly moulds, pewter tea sets, copper saucepans. He brought it all back with a few surprises.

However, his biggest surprise came when it was my turn to go to England. One morning, as I sat in the breakfast room of the Edwardian hotel facing the British Museum, the waitress brought me a letter from David. I picked up the butter knife to open the envelop and noticed a message written on the outside under the flap, an after-thought. "I have bought the house."

Within three years of opening our business, he purchased an 1882 Victorian house which has been our home for over forty years and where our memories surround us.

We have been retired for over ten years at the time of writing, yet we meet customers daily who remember the store and inevitably ask,

"Do you miss it?"

I reply "Not really."

Former customers share anecdotes in the most unlikely spots. A few days ago, as I sat wearing a blue cotton tie-on gown in the endoscopy admitting area of St. Joseph's Hospital, a bare legged gentleman in the same attire sitting opposite asked, "Did you have a kitchen store?"

"Yes, but we've been retired for over ten years now."

"Well, we're not likely to forget Ann McColl's. My wife and I credit you for keeping us together. Remember those slatted wooden dish racks? We shared one from your place before we married and argued over who should get it if we broke up. We decided to marry so that we could both keep it. Our children, now in their twenties, help us to slot the china into that same rack."

I consider this a satisfactory legacy.

RECIPE INDEX

Soups
   Market Minstrone, 105

Vegetarian Options
   Art-Inspired Vegetable Side Dish, 84
   Bistro Lentils, 17
   Braised Leeks in Crème Fraîche, 26
   Jewel Coucous Salad, 29
   Rice and Squash Gratin, 35
   Salade Niçoise, 69
   Swiss Cheese Fondue, 154

ACKNOWLEDGMENTS

Raise a glass:

To Benedict Lockwood, who brought his European background knowledge to the chapters on Switzerland, Austria and Germany.

To a valued Danish friend and neighbour, Ulla Troughton, who shared her personal experiences of Copenhagen with us.

To Thelma Sumsion and Helen Luckman, who scoured the entire first draft, deleting copious spelling errors. If any are left, I added them later.

To London's core independent book stores:

Attic Books	Oxford Books
240 Dundas Street	262 Piccadilly Street
London N6A 1H3	London N6A 1S4

They have sold our previous books:

The Cookshop Cookbook 1974
Ann McColl's 25 Greatest Hits 1994
Store Animals 2007
Hungry Hearts 2011

And surely it's the luck of the Irish to live two doors away from Grace, Joe, Linda and Mike O'Connor. They make books.

CPSIA information can be obtained at www.ICGtesting.com
Printed in the USA
LVOW090400240212

270146LV00006B/1/P